# Education Research for Teachers, School Leaders, and Administrators

## Using Data and Research as a Tool for Equitable Practice

*Preliminary Edition*

Irina S. Okhremtchouk, PhD.
Marta del Valle Induni, PhD.
Vincent C. Matthews, EdD.
*San Francisco State University*

Cover © Shutterstock.com

www.kendallhunt.com
*Send all inquiries to:*
4050 Westmark Drive
Dubuque, IA 52004-1840

Copyright © 2022 by Kendall Hunt Publishing Company

ISBN: 978-1-7924-9695-0

All rights reserved. No part of this publication may be reproduced, stored in a retrieval system, or transmitted, in any form or by any means, electronic, mechanical, photocopying, recording, or otherwise, without the prior written permission of the copyright owner.

Published in the United States of America

# CONTENTS

*Foreword* ................................................................................................ v

*Preface* ................................................................................................. ix

*Author Bios* ........................................................................................... xi

**Chapter 1**  Educational Research as a Tool for Better Informed School Practices ............................................................................. 1
*How can research help inform my leadership and pedagogical practices?*

**Chapter 2**  The Basics: Review of Concepts in Research ........................... 11
*Where do I start?*

**Chapter 3**  The Stepping Stones of Data-informed Practice: Academic Literature Search, Literature Review & Annotated Bibliography ............................................................ 25
*Now that I have a topic, where do I look?*

**Chapter 4**  Quantitative Research and Application ................................ 37
*When and how do I use quantitative research to understand school practices?*

**Chapter 5**  Qualitative Research and Application .................................. 49
*When and how do I use qualitative research to inform school practices?*

**Chapter 6**  Mixed-methods Research and Application ..................................61
*What are the effective ways to utilize qualitative and quantitative research to deepen understanding about school leadership and pedagogical practices?*

**Chapter 7**  Data Fluency: The Foundations of Quantitative and Qualitative Data Analysis ..................................71
*Now that I completed data collection, what do I do?*

**Chapter 8**  Formulating a Problem Statement: Key Elements in Academic Writing and Research Direction ..................................85
*Now what? Data collected, analysis completed, what's next?*

**Chapter 9**  Research Leading to Better Informed Practice: Action Research ..................................97
*What research method provides tools for practical application that I can employ to investigate my own practice or use with a community of educators?*

**Chapter 10**  Research Leading to Better Informed Practice: Survey Research ..................................103
*Now that I completed my initial research and formulated a problem statement, how do I learn from my education community to make change possible and further engage in cycle of inquiry?*

**Chapter 11**  Research Leading to Better Informed Practice: Single-Case Research ..................................113
*What research method provides tools for practical application that I can use to learn whether an intervention is effective?*

**Chapter 12**  Well-informed Decisions Lead to Better Outcomes: Research as a Tool for Educators, Education Leaders, and Administrators ..................................121

# FOREWORD

**Henry Tran, PhD,** Associate Professor at the University of South Carolina's Department of Educational Leadership and Policies

Dr. Henry Tran is an Associate Professor at the University of South Carolina's Department of Educational Leadership and Policies who studies issues related to education human resources (HR) and finance. He holds two national HR certifications and serves on the Board of Advisors and Board of Trustees for the National Education Finance Academy. He is also the editor of the *Journal of Education Human Resources* and the Director of the **Talent Centered Education Leadership Initiative**, and lead editor of the forthcoming book: *How Did We Get Here? The Decay of the Teaching Profession.*

## *Foreword* by Henry Tran MPA, SHRM-CP, PHR, PhD

Since the landmark report "A Nation at Risk: The Imperative for Educational Reform" was published in 1983, accountability has been at the forefront of the education policy discussions. Schools were increasingly asked to adopt evidence-based practices, implement standards-based reform initiatives, make research-based decisions, and regularly report data on their student performance. Federal legislation and incentive efforts such as *No Child Left Behind, Race to the Top,* and Every *Student Succeeds Act* continued to emphasize these efforts.

Because of the way that education accountability has been emphasized, it can be easy to view education research and data solely for compliance purposes, as a way to respond to governmental and public demands. While it can serve that purpose, they can be so much more. It is increasingly understood that a sole reliance on research and data associated with "what works" for improving student test scores, is overly narrow and ignores other valuable sources of data including educators' personal observation and understanding "why a policy or an intervention failed so we can improve our next attempt" (Gordon & Conaway, 2020, p. 1). Mandinach and Schildkamp (2021) explain that the field's emphasis has evolved from

> a focus on one source of data (standardized assessment data) and one outcome measure (student achievement) to the use of a variety of data sources (e.g., classroom observations, student voice data, parent surveys) and broad range of outcome measures (e.g., student achievement, student learning, wellbeing) (p. 1).

As time progressed, the realization of the limitations of an overly singular focus on student learning outcomes (primarily defined by standardized achievement scores) has led to calls for more diversity in the type of data collected including school level expenditure and school climate data.

Beyond technical rigor, data and research must also be balanced with relevance to practitioners if they are to have practical application. In fact, there has been a shift in the paradigm of the promotion of data use from summative assessment style data that are meant to demonstrate compliance with accountability, to formative style assessments that are designed to promote continuous learning improvement that are responsive to the needs of each individual student (Mandinach & Schildkamp, 2021).

Moreover, data should inform decision-making but should not dictate it. Other practical considerations such as experiential, political, and financial factors should be considered alongside data-based evidence to aid leaders in their decision-making. Indeed, as Okhremtchouk, Induni, and Matthews (the authors of this book) stress, research can serve as a valuable *tool* for educational practice. For example, with data and evidence, inequity can be documented. Problems can be highlighted so that stakeholders can know that solutions are needed and work with the data to inform the design of those solutions. Without systematized data and evidence, decision makers can fall into the trap of relying solely on their subjective assumptions, opinions, and "gut feelings" on how to proceed (e.g., overly relying on assumptions made concerning why students are underperforming, opinions on why staff and faculty morale is low, and feelings about why schools continue to see underrepresentation of teachers from particular demographics), which is inevitably clouded by personal bias. The education leaders of today increasingly understand the risks associated with such actions. While most decision makers have long relied at least some sort of data to inform their decisions (Mandinach, 2012), unfortunately, as Gordon and Conway (2020) explain, many are not trained to evaluate the validity of research evidence to determine its trustworthiness to base their actions on, and are therefore more prone to be influenced by weak and nonsystematized data that support the leaders' preexisting beliefs and promote confirmatory bias in their decisions.

Even in the broader community outside of education, data informed decision-making has become increasingly ubiquitous. Just think about how many companies collect data (indirect data tracking) on users during their Internet searches to produce target and tailor advertisements for them. Businesses can collect data about their customers who visit their website and social media outlets to identify trends, demographics, behaviors, and more to inform their next action steps. Retailers can track inventory stock with data to ensure the supply of goods is replenished before they become empty. In addition, organizations often distribute surveys to and conduct focus groups with their client base to (directly) receive feedback on their services in order to help improve future operations.

What these constellation of events in both education and the broader community means for schools and their leaders is that there is an increasing expectation for the application of research and data for their decision-making. This should not come as a surprise. Leaders influence people and modern approaches in the field of people management (aka Human Resources/Talent management, an area of expertise of mine) have increasingly advocated for the promotion of a data informed decision-making culture, with iterative testing and learning to respond to employee feedback and input. In fact, not only is data sought after in a general sense, but

> evidence-based talent management decisions require more and more data on an individual basis in real time to find out what employees really care about right now. Tapping into this ambient people data in order to make predictive statements about the workforce is becoming an integral part of the new talent management order (Claus, 2019, p. 209).

The utilization of data to inform decision-making is so critical, that I identified it as one of the seven core principles in my customization of cutting-edge progressive people management for education, which I call Talent-centered Education Leadership (Tran & Jenkins, 2022). The rationale is that education employee data provides a mechanism for school employers to truly understand their employee needs and solicit their input and ideas, in order to aide employers in designing engaging employee experiences for their workers during their time in the organization. This is particularly relevant in the context of educator (e.g., teachers and administrators) and school staff shortages, that are primarily fueled by turnover. In fact, looking back at the long-standing history of teacher shortages and turnover, D'Amico Pawlewicz (2021) notes that "Teachers have long explained what they need to stay. Unless administrators, school boards and communities start listening, the pattern repeating itself again today will continue to rear its ugly head" (para 18), and research and data is one mechanism that allows for that deep systematic "listening" to occur.

In sum, data literacy (i.e., the ability and capacity of individuals to use data to develop actionable knowledge to inform strategies and decisions) is increasingly important and required for education leaders. The authors of the book take their readers on the journey toward gaining this very important skill that can be used to satisfy the summative and formative needs of educational institutions.

## References

Claus, L. (2019). HR disruption—Time already to reinvent talent management. *BRQ Business Research Quarterly*, 22(3), 207–215.

D'Amico Pawlewicz, D. (2021). *Today's teacher shortages are part of a longer pattern*. The Washington Post. https://www.washingtonpost.com/outlook/2021/11/18/todays-teacher-shortages-are-part-longer-pattern/

Gordon, N., & Conaway, C. (2020). *Common-sense evidence: The education leader's guide to using data and research. The Educational Innovation Series*. Harvard Education Press.

Mandinach, E. B. (2012). A perfect time for data use: Using data-driven decision making to inform practice. *Educational Psychologist, 47*(2), 71–85.

Mandinach, E. B., & Schildkamp, K. (2021). The complexity of data-based decision making: An introduction to the special issue. *Studies in Educational Evaluation, 69*, 100906.

Tran, H., & Jenkins. (2022). Embracing the future of education work with talent centered education leadership. *Journal of Education Human Resources*. In Press.

# PREFACE

> "How in the world could this class possibly contribute to my pedagogical practice or inform my leadership actions? I'm dreading Educational Research Seminar class, but it's required, agh!"
>
> – *Anonymous Graduate Program in Education Candidate*

Sentiments such as the one quoted above about educational research seminars—often a required course in graduate programs—are commonplace. This text, *Education Research for Educators, School Leaders, and Administrators: Using Data as a Tool for Equitable Practice*, is designed to address the very question posed by the candidate in the quote above.

We (the authors) are both practitioners and academicians in the field of education. While some of us are more immersed in practice than academics and vice versa, we all use research as a *tool* in our careers to guide our decision-making, and add new knowledge to the extant literature. We also serve as faculty in higher education, teaching research courses along with the educational leadership and administration subjects.

As an associate professor of education (Irina), a researcher in a nonprofit sector (Marta), and a superintendent of schools (Vincent), we share many interests and values relating to the field of education and educational research. It is not an overstatement to say that foremost among our values are commitment, dedication, and passion for social justice, racial equity, and lessening disparities in the education system. We are committed to progress since progress is a necessary evolutionary component of education. We believe that the informed utilization of research is essential to making progress possible, improving practice, and adding to the field's evidence-based resources.

After many shared years of teaching and designing Education Research courses along with professional development for practitioners, we wanted to create a pathway to demystify existing education data and teach students methodologies they will most likely use. In our conversations about how education research is introduced and taught in academic settings, we continuously stressed a need for an application component that would allow candidates (our students) to integrate research methods into practice as they learn about these methods—an approach often lacking in the existing introductory research methods textbooks and courses.

While discussing how to fill this "practical application" gap in our classes, it became increasingly clear that the field needs a text that simultaneously introduces and integrates research methods concepts into practice. Because we work with teachers, educators, and education leaders who intend to continue on the path of school leadership, we used the new California Administrator Performance Assessment (CalAPA) requirement of engaging with data to improve school site practice as an inspiration for this textbook.

## Preface

We embedded assignments alongside chapters to align with various methodologies. This allows candidates to authentically engage with the content, including fulfilling one of the CalAPA requirements. As such, this text is the consequence of our many conversations about how to fill the practical application gap in Education Research Seminar courses, as well as our way of addressing not only graduate program candidates' requirements, but also interests that they can put into practice for years to come.

In a nutshell, our overarching goal for this introductory text is simple: *By making research methods more accessible and applicable, educators will come to view and use research as a* **tool** *to improve practice.*

For all of the above reasons, we wrote this text in a relatable, approachable manner while constantly placing ourselves in our students' shoes.

As we conceptualized each chapter, application engagement, and assignment, we did it with you (our reader) in mind. In doing so, our aim is to create thoughtful, logical content to guide you through real-world data application. Whether you are an aspiring teacher, educator, educational leader, or preparing to be a school administrator, as you engage with this textbook, you will be introduced to and learn about how to utilize research methods and data in your practice. Put differently, the approach of applying research as a *tool* will open the gateway of using research in practice for better, more robust decision-making, be it in a classroom where you teach, at a department meeting that you lead, or while guiding an education community as part of your administrative responsibilities.

We also need to mention what this book is not. This text is not designed to explore complex data analysis in education research. For any complex, in-depth exploration of a specific research method, you would need to take specialized coursework outside of the typical Seminar in Education Research introductory course to master these skills.

Finally, as you begin your learning journey with the help of this textbook, we sincerely hope that using data and research as a *tool* will help you make informed, evidence-based decisions and, therefore, impact many lives of young people for the better through practices that respect students' humanity and afford them an environment supportive of their strengths.

Happy learning!
*Irina, Marta, & Vincent*

# AUTHOR BIOS

## IRINA S. OKHREMTCHOUK, PhD.

### Dr. Irina Okhremtchouk, *Associate Professor, San Francisco State University*

Dr. Okhremtchouk is an associate professor of educational administration in the Department of Equity, Leadership Studies, and Instructional Technologies at San Francisco State University's (SFSU) Graduate College of Education. She also coordinates SFSU's educational administration certification and MA programs. In her capacity as program coordinator, Dr. Okhremtchouk is charged with preparing well-rounded and well-informed equity-driven school leaders and administrators who are ready to build and maintain inclusive school communities, as well as work persistently to eliminate racism, inequalities, and injustices. Okhremtchouk's research and expertise are in school organization, policy, and finance. Specifically, her scholarly work stems from a deep interest in translating research into better-informed public policy and practice yielding a long-lasting impact on school leadership, administration, and better-informed teaching.

## MARTA INDUNI, PhD.

### Dr. Marta Induni, *Researcher*

Born in Argentina and a native Spanish speaker, Marta Induni, PhD, has held progressive leadership roles in public health for over 30 years, and prior to joining Adventist Health served as Senior Director of Research with the Public Health Institute. Dr. Induni received her doctoral degree in Educational Psychology from the University of California, Davis, where she studied health behavior change theory, prevention, resilience, and intervention programs for adolescents.

With a quest for knowledge and learning, each opportunity expanded her through the design of research studies, responding to grant opportunities, and collaborating with organizations on the leading edge of research, disease control, and securing funding. Working with large data collection programs has kindled a deep interest in health data and clinical informatics. With special attention to actionable research designed to improve health outcomes and health equity, Dr. Induni is also a certified informaticist.

Dr. Induni enjoys teaching education research and mentoring graduate students in the Department of Equity, Leadership Studies, & Instructional Technologies at San Francisco State University. She enjoys traveling with her teenaged daughters, and gardening and curating an eclectic Frida Kahlo-inspired collection.

# VINCENT C. MATTHEWS, EdD.

## Dr. Vincent Matthews, *Superintendent*

As superintendent of the San Francisco Unified School District (SFUSD), Dr. Vincent Matthews is the top executive of the eighth largest school district in California and the third largest employer in San Francisco. Guided by Vision 2025, a blueprint for the future of public education in San Francisco and the strategic *plan Impact Learning, Impact Lives*, SFUSD has continued to accomplish major results under Dr. Matthews' leadership.

A native of San Francisco, Vincent Matthews completed his pre-K-12 education as a student at William DeAvila, formally Dudley Stone ECE, Grattan Elementary, Hoover Middle, and JE McAteer High School. Following graduation from McAteer, Matthews earned his Bachelor of Arts, Teaching Credential, Masters, and eventually his doctorate in Education from San Francisco State University. Early in his career as an educator he taught at George Washington Carver Elementary School and served as principal at Alvarado Elementary School, John Muir Middle School in San Leandro, and Edison Elementary.

Before the San Francisco Board of Education selected Dr. Matthews to serve as superintendent, Dr. Matthews served the California Department of Education as the state-appointed superintendent of Inglewood Unified School District. Prior to serving in Inglewood, Matthews led the San Jose Unified School District as superintendent for 5 1/2 years where he is credited with raising academic achievement, narrowing the achievement gap between Latino and White students, and passing landmark agreements with the San Jose Teacher's union. Prior to working in San Jose, he served as a state-appointed superintendent for Oakland Unified and as an area superintendent for San Diego City Schools.

# CHAPTER 1

# Educational Research as a Tool for Better Informed School Practices

*How can research help inform my leadership and pedagogical practices?*

## 1.1 | Introduction

In this chapter, we introduce our central argument for this textbook—the importance of viewing and using **research** as a *tool* in education settings. As we present our argument in this chapter, we discuss the significance of inquiry, how research can assist you in your practice, and review the practical application of research through examples of published research articles authored by practitioners. Finally, we conclude this chapter with discussion questions and an interactive exercise.

> "Research is to see what everybody has seen and think what nobody has thought."
> 
> —Albert Szent-Gyorgyi

## 1.2 | Shifting the Paradigm: Using Research as a *Tool*

An educational research class is typically *that class* that everyone dreads in graduate school, their teacher preparation program, or leadership training. This class is usually met with the sentiment of "why do I need this?" or "how in the world a quasi-experimental design could possibly contribute to my pedagogical practice or inform my leadership actions?" It is not unheard of that many students even dread the thought of an educational research class thinking, "this is way too hard, complicated and boring." If these thoughts are echoing in your mind, then this is your lucky day—because we are here to flip your thinking about education research. It would be safe to say students rarely appreciate that an educational research class can be considered a *tool* for better-informed decision-making, better informed pedagogical practice, and better-informed leadership, among other possible uses.

That is right, we just said it—research is a *tool* and not some remote, unachievable set of never-to-be-used concepts or protocols. This said, we know that is not how this topic is typically relayed or presented—we have been there and done that. All three of us, Marta, Vincent, and Irina had gone through extensive research training in our MA programs and later PhD and EDD, all to find out before embarking on our dissertations (when doing primary research is an actual requirement) that research, and educational research in particular, is a *TOOL*! What a discovery. This is also when we learned that not only it is a tool, but in fact an invaluable set of skills that became paramount in everything that we do. So now, as university professors working with educators, educator–leaders, and aspiring administrators we are doing our best to pass-on this invaluable *tool* to up-and-coming candidates learning about educational research with a major focus on utility and utilization of data to improve practice. In other words, we aim to change this perspective by first acknowledging the obvious and then unpacking research in the way that is both engaging and practical.

The research component focusing on data science in education has been expanding ever since the start of this century and especially after No Child Left Behind (NCLB). With the passage of NCLB in 2002, evidence-based practices and highly qualified teachers became synonymous with progress and school improvement. But how do we ensure evidence-based practices work, especially in your own unique context and circumstances? How can we be certain that highly qualified teachers know how to address diverse student needs in their classrooms and sustain as well as expand on their professional capital to continue to be highly qualified both in the field and within their own unique education communities? How can school site leaders and administrators, that are responsible for a quarter of schools' success with respect to student achievement (Leithwood et al., 2004), effectively engage in examining school's progress to determine the next steps? How do we know what works and what does not? Is intuition, professional preparation, and (perhaps) experience enough to get a trained professional through? How do we balance the time between professional obligations and engaging in inquiry about our own practice?

It is true that good intuition and training are foundational for any profession, but considering the needs of a 21st-century classroom, a set of skills that would lead to ongoing expansion of professional capital is necessary (Hargreaves & Fullan, 2012). As we make our case here for educational research to be used as a tool, it begs a reminder of how our schools are evolving.

There is little debate that contemporary public schools in the U.S. embody diversity and are becoming more and more diverse every day. As student demographics and identities diversify, so are the needs students bring into a classroom. Therefore, informed knowledge and good data are necessary to inform meaningful pedagogical and leadership practices, especially where intuition, common sense, and even experience can only provide limited insight into ever expanding student needs. That is where, we argue, the knowledge of how to engage in research is necessary.

The knowledge to be able to read, analyze, and work with data; The knowledge to reflect and communicate findings; The ability to embark on well-designed investigations; and the ability to tie specific findings and data to a school site or classroom to make better-informed decisions. Having a solid understanding about educational research and the many benefits it offers is the way forward. Understanding data and the ability to collect, organize, and analyze these data—even in the simplest descriptive ways—will provide much insight for educators, educator leaders, and site administrators.

As the field of data science is certainly becoming a necessity for any given field, the field of education is no exception. From school districts, to school sites, to individual classrooms, data-driven and data-informed practices are at the forefront of all and any conversations having to do with education. So, what does it take to have education research in your tool-kit and own it as a skill? Our answer is simple: interest and commitment. Throughout this textbook, and this chapter in particular we will attempt to capture both: your interest and your commitment.

## 1.3 | Inquiry as a Starting Point

To make research possible, one must be open to engage in inquiry. What we are emphasizing here is that inquiry into practices within the field of education is necessary to get started. In fact, inquiry is not only necessary, but it is also synonymous with the scientific method, which is a guide for anyone doing research no matter the scale of the project. We will unpack the scientific method in more detail in the next chapter (Chapter 2); our aim for this section is to focus on inquiry first as means of what is to come.

> Once we lose the desire to understand—to be surprised, to listen and bear witness—we lose our humanity. Among the most important capacities that you take with you today is your curiosity. You must guard it, for curiosity is the beginning of empathy.—Atul Gawande [Quote from New Yorker,

June 2, 2018 "*Curiosity and What Equality Really Means,*" commencement address at U.C.L.A. Medical School.

Inquiry requires several components. The first of which is a topic or interest in a topic that would essentially evolve into a question. The second requirement is the research toolbox—a systematic approach or way of thinking and organizing that follows steps to construct research building blocks: necessary actions to learn about a topic and allow for an investigation to answer that question with an intent to arrive closer to the truth, *hopefully*. If you have not noticed, we did italicize *hopefully*, and here is why. It is absolutely expected that an answer to the question you pose as a part of your inquiry will lead to many more questions and many more inquiries! The questions and topics are likely to shift as you learn more about your subject of interest. This is expected and clearly represents the cycle of inquiry. It is continuous, ongoing, and although not always required, often times needs reengagement, especially when one engages in research that is applied.

One of the methods for this cycle of inquiry is called action research. In Chapter 9, we unpack action research in much detail, but we do want to mention it here since the notion of action research and its practical, cyclical nature of first inquiring, then planning, then implementing, and finally analyzing and reflecting serves as a foundation. That is, a foundation to inquire about one's own leadership or pedagogical practices. Action research is also a base for the cycle of inquiry that we will unpack in Chapter 9. Likewise, many state and national assessments from EdTPA (Teacher Performance Assessment) to CalAPA (California Administrator Performance Assessment) and Teacher National Board Certification all rely on the cycle of inquiry where the four tasks: (1) Investigate, (2) Plan, (3) Act, and (4) Reflect are the progression components for these performance assessments the concept for which is derived from action research: a systemic way of approaching a problem or addressing a practical need to enact a study of one's own practice or that with a community of practice centered on a goal to improve practice for better outcomes, be it instruction or leadership.

## 1.4 | How Can Research Help Inform My Leadership and Pedagogical Practice?

Now that we introduced the concept of inquiry, our hope is twofold, to capture your interests and to help answer the following question: *How can research help inform my leadership and pedagogical practice*? In the next section, we will discuss practical application of research and provide examples of how research can be used as a *tool* in practice. In doing so, these excerpts from published studies offer a window into how practitioners engage in research to better their professional practice. Likewise, these selected studies serve as examples of steps practitioner–researchers undertake, from choosing a topic, posing a question to a data collection process, documentation of results, and discussion of findings. We purposefully made these selections so you could see yourselves engaging in similar work. Although your needs and interests in the type of research might differ from the examples presented below, these works provide a starting point for utilizing research as a *tool*. Whether you investigate what makes a difference in your own classroom, your department, or how your equity-driven leadership practices influence a school's culture, all play a role in an expansion of your professional capital and moving closer to well-informed, data-driven decision-making.

As we continue to stress the importance of using research whether it is from the perspective outside the school or from the perspective of a school leader or from a classroom teacher, one must ultimately understand that using research must be connected to the importance of answering three main school improvement process questions with the first being the most important:

1. What are we trying to improve? How do we stay disciplined in using data to identify gaps and opportunities? [This question is asked pre-research/pre-inquiry]

2. What changes might we make or actions might we continue and why? We draw from research to answer this question. [This question is posed post-research to assist with application]
3. And finally, how will we know if changes or actions lead to improvement? This is where accountability plays a key role. In other words, measuring impact helps us learn what is working and what is not working in serving students and addressing unique needs they bring into a classroom, especially students who have been historically and habitually underserved. [This question is asked post-research when reflecting on evidence]

> **Food for Thought** With a peer or in a small group, discuss why research allows practitioners to make informed decisions that will lead to effectively answering all three questions listed above?

## 1.5 | Application: Research in Practice

It is time to take a closer look at examples of empirical research. We often read about someone doing research on "us" or our field or our students, our schools, our districts, and so on, but we rarely know about or engage with work that is done by practitioners about their own practice on the topic that they care about or care to know about and document. In this section, we highlight literature and provide excerpts from published research that has been done by practitioners in hopes of giving you insights into what is possible in a form of examples. We cover three distinct topics starting with a larger context that extends beyond the classroom and into the community, then we include a research article that looks into instruction practices that are designed to address student well-being and, lastly, we selected a piece that covers best practices for school site leadership as they implement positive behavior interventions. It is our hope that these examples, excerpts from research articles, serve to inspire you to engage in inquiry where you can begin thinking about your own possible topics for investigation as we continue to outline the tools necessary to do so throughout this text.

### Outside of Classroom

As we think about how collaboration occurs to improve practice, we selected to showcase this research article for several reasons. One, it encompasses action research forums (more on action research in Chapter 9) as the way to collect data and engage in research of practice. Two, the study is unique since it bridges multiple silos and practices by engaging university faculty, school community, families, and the larger community to improve teacher preparation by authentically determining inclusive practices. Three, both the method used (i.e., action research) and the topic of this study should be of interest to educational leaders, be it teachers or administrators, since this work offers a valuable *tool* in conducting research to improve practice. Likewise, this work provides a foundation for ways into how school site professional development could be improved to represent a multi-silo perspective. That is, the same method of collaboration through forums may be adapted to design professional development for teachers and staff at school sites. This research article in its entirety can be found through an open-source journal by selecting the citation provided below. For the purposes of learning, here we present selected sections of the research study: an abstract, introduction, the methods section, and findings to familiarize you with the key aspects of the research.

## School, University, and Community Collaboration to Promote Equity through Inclusive Cultural Competence

*Tammy Ellis-Robinson*
*&*
*Jessica Wayde-Coles*
*University at Albany*

**Citation**: Ellis-Robinson, T., & Wayde-Coles, J. (2021). School, university and community collaboration to promote equity through inclusive cultural competence. *Education Policy Analysis Archives, 29*(44). https://doi.org/10.14507/epaa.29.4670 This article is part of the Special Issue, *Striving for Social Justice and Equity in Higher Education,* guest edited by Irina Okhremtchuk, Caroline Turner, & Patrick Newell.

### Abstract

In a series of action-research forums university researchers/faculty, school, family, and community stakeholders engaged collaboratively to explore and identify effective practices and ongoing needs related to the development of inclusive cultural competence for preservice and in-service teachers, and the institutions that develop and employ them. Forum participants discussed plans for future collaborative projects focused on equity and social justice in local schools and community organizations. The collaborative relationships extended beyond the forums to include additional projects focused on equity. Researchers used a qualitative analysis of forum input and researcher field notes, including deductive category application of codes derived from literature and modeling of intersections of theory and forum output to identify problem areas, analyze themes of best practice, and formulate ideas for future action.

### Conclusion

The forums have led to an ongoing collaboration and conversation among and between the stakeholders at each forum, and a growing network of colleagues and additional stakeholders. This has led to the development of several actions derived from the initial set of forums. Actions include an annual Equity in Transition Summit for many more stakeholders in the process as well as the establishment of a Facebook page and Listserv to encourage ongoing collaboration in the provision of equitable practice. Other ongoing actions include professional development for supervisors of preservice teachers, professional development in action research and cultural competence, an online book discussion, a middle school case study and action research project, collaborative planning, a survey of special educators perceptions of self-efficacy for intersectional issues, revisions of preservice teacher curricular focus, and additional forums. The forums have provided an opportunity to build momentum in a collaborative community across institutions and anchored in the local community. Follow up forums have included brainstorming of new initiatives and ideas for further development with innovations for inclusive equitable practice in mind. Several of the participating districts-initiated policies to enact explorations and conversations like those in the forums within their institutions. Through collaboration, action, and with an eye toward social justice collaborative efforts can promote equity in practice among teachers and within institutional policy.

### In the Classroom

As education leaders, both teachers and administrators grapple with educating the "whole child," we thought to include excerpts from a research article on this very subject. This article is particularly timely since it is not only done by practitioners, but was set to investigate one of the most talked-about areas in education, mindfulness. The research is a good example of how a practitioner, a first-grade teacher, can employ research methods as a *tool* to look into whether the practice of mindfulness strengthens self-efficacy among her students. This study used a mixed-method approach (more on Mixed-Methods in Chapter 6) to examine how daily mindfulness practices can influence students' social-emotional skills and resiliency. As we present the key excerpts of this study for the learning purposes, the full article can be found through a full citation included below.

## Does Mindfulness Strengthen Self Efficacy in First Grade Students?

*Kirsten L. Logan,*
*First grade teacher*
*&*
*Erik K. Laursen*
*University of Richmond*

Logan, K. L., & Laursen, E. K. (2019). Does mindfulness strengthen self-efficacy in first grade students? *The Journal of Teacher Action Research, 6*(1), 32–43. http://www.practicalteacherresearch.com/uploads/5/6/2/4/56249715/does_mindfulness_strengthen_self-_efficacy_in_first_grade_students.pdf

### Abstract

External and internal stressors often influence young children's sense of self-efficacy and resiliency negatively. Practicing mindfulness within the classroom may be one intervention that can help students strengthen the social-emotional skills involved in self-efficacy and resiliency. This study used a mixed method approach to gather quantitative and qualitative data from six first-grade students who participated in a daily mindfulness practice. The data were analyzed using descriptive statistics to determine if their perceptions of self-efficacy and resiliency improved from week one to week six of the study. Logico-inductive data analyses were used to identify common themes in student interviews. Students favored the mindfulness activities and shared benefits such as feeling calm, happy, and a sense of self-control. The six-week timeframe and small sample size are possible limitations for this research study to show significant differences through the quantitative data analysis.

### Conclusion

We encourage school leaders to provide teachers who are willing and ready to take on the incorporation of mindfulness practices with professional development on being a "mindful leader." There are professional development workshops and online classes that can be utilized for teachers to become familiar with different programs and mindfulness activities. Teachers who practice and familiarize themselves with mindfulness first will have a smoother transition implementing it within their own classroom.

Finally, we suggest that teachers reflect on students' perceptions of mindfulness activities and the impact on students' self-efficacy and resiliency. Follow-up research on ways to measure student perceptions of mindfulness practices is suggested to best fit the age group of students who are participating in mindfulness practices.

### In the School

As we think about effective school administrative practices, we must consider student discipline. The topic and practice of Positive Behavior Interventions and Supports (PBIS) has been widely implemented throughout school districts. In this section, we present excerpts from a qualitative study (more on

Qualitative Research in Chapter 5) conducted by practitioners with the main purpose to use research as a *tool* in examining what constitutes best PBIS practices. This study is designed to serve as a practical resource to inform both teacher leaders and school administrators on best PBIS practices. As we highlight key excerpts of the study, the complete article can be downloaded through a full citation provided below.

## Best Practice PBIS Implementation: Evidence Indicators in Each Tier of the PBIS Champion Model

*Jessica Djabrayan Hannigan,*
*California State University, Fresno, CA*
*&*
*John Hannigan,*
*Office of Fresno County Superintendent of Schools, Fresno, CA*

Djabrayan-Hannigan, J., & Hannigan, J. (2020). Best practice PBIS implementation: Evidence indicators in each tier of PBIS champion model. *Journal of School Administration Research and Development, 4*(1), 35–38. https://www.ojed.org/index.php/JSARD/article/view/2111/1028

### Abstract

This study presents empirical data on the best practice implementation of the Positive Behavior Interventions and Supports (PBIS) Champion Model in schools at each of the three tiers of implementation. The purpose of this study was to identify PBIS best practice evidence indicators for each of the tiers. The design included a review of evidence indicators from a cohort of schools ($N = 117$) that participated in a three-year PBIS Champion Model workshop series during the 2016 to 2019 school years and met model criteria for implementation based on the PBIS Champion Model Framework. Evidence indicators were collected and analyzed from schools that met the requirements of each implementation level. While some met the requirements of all three levels, others met those of two, one, or none. Of the 117 schools in the cohort, 113 schools met the Tier 1 level (Bronze) requirement, 94 met the Tier 2 level (Silver) requirement, and 86 met the Tier 3 level (Gold) requirement. The findings indicate a variety of evidence indicators in each tier of the PBIS Champion Model Framework (i.e., processes, protocols, trainings, communication structures) that aligns with Deming's Plan, Do, Study, Act (PDSA) cycle for quality implementation. This study presents a practical resource that can guide successful systemic implementation of PBIS in each tier and can support student academic learning and behavior in those schools.

### Discussion and Recommendations

Our recommendations for implementation success are framed around Edward Deming's Plan, Do, Study, Act (PDSA) cycle (Tague, 2015). The PDSA cycle is an effective organizational change management model utilized with teams across a variety of domains, and it is often used to help teams improve the quality of implementation. The first step, *plan*, is often defined as a process for a team to ensure alignment of aims and goals. The second step, *do*, is defined as a process for teams to implement their plan. The third step, *study*, is often defined as a process for teams to study effectiveness and analyze the results of their plan based on relevant data. The fourth step, *act*, is defined as a process for teams to adjust or modify the plan to improve implementation based on their findings. The evidence indicators from each tier in this study can be best implemented using the PDSA cycle as a framework. In each tier, there are identified evidence indicators for PBIS teams that align with the *plan, do, study*, and *act* stages. In fact, all of the evidence indicators reveal the importance of having a designated group of local experts that know their goals, roles, and responsibilities and have a structure in place for analyzing the behavior data for the students and adjusting goals based on student and stakeholder needs on an ongoing basis.

When implementation stagnates, we recommend that educators examine whether or not their actions in each tier address two important elements: (1) the collection of evidence of implementation effectiveness and (2) the use of the PDSA cycle of implementation improvement. If they do not, it likely indicates a misalignment of implementation. Subsequently, the designated team in each tier should revisit the *plan* to ensure the alignment is adjusted and stakeholders involved understand the steps to move implementation (i.e., the area of focus—tiered implementation of PBIS) back in alignment with its common goals.

Too often, schools lack evidence of PBIS implementation—particularly in the area of student-needs-aligned implementation in each tier. Therefore, it is critical for educators doing this work to not only know how to identify the evidence of effectiveness of this work, but most importantly to understand that implementation in each tier requires an organizational structure to ensure ongoing effectiveness and sustainability of implementation. Although the three research questions of this study were used to examine the best practice indicators in each tier, we encourage practitioners to systematize their processes for ongoing success. Without this systemization, schools often experience a breakdown in implementation as teams in each tier are adjusted and restructured or as new leaders are assigned to a school or team. The PBIS Champion Model can assist as an organizational frame that aligns with the PDSA cycle, and it can ensure ongoing implementation success if each tier of the framework is followed with full fidelity and accountability structures are established and maintained.

## 1.6 | Conclusion

Using research as a tool to make informed decisions about one's own professional practice, be it pedagogical or leadership, is paramount. Considering the burgeoning diversity of our student population and the unique needs they bring into a contemporary classroom, engaging in research is not only good practice but is necessary for any given practice to be effective.

Twenty-five percent of school success is depended upon school's leadership and its administrators. In fact, school site "leadership is second only to classroom instruction among all school-related factors that contribute to what students learn at school" (Leithwood et al., 2004, p. 5). Although evidence about leadership effects on student learning can be at time convoluted to interpret, much of the existing research underestimates its effects. This evidence supports the present widespread interest in improving school site leadership as a key component to the successful implementation of large-scale reform (Wallace, 2021). This highlights the importance of school leaders and administrators making data-informed and data-driven decisions—said differently, using research as a *tool* to improve leadership practices.

In a classroom, the instructional practices—the teacher—is the one single factor that could make a difference in the academic trajectories of their students. A positive teacher-instruction impact could lead to lifelong benefits for the students. The second excerpt above, a study done by a first-grade teacher, highlights the impact of and importance of instruction practices that focus on student well-being. Similarly, the study serves as an example of how teachers can introduce an intervention, gather data, and then make data-driven decisions.

It is our hope that as you conclude reading this chapter, you are now more open to the concept that research is not just something used in graduate education courses, but a valuable *tool* that should be incorporated by educator leaders and educators to assist in the critical decisions made on a daily, weekly, monthly, and annual basis. The ultimate question that should constantly be on your mind is, *what are we trying to improve?* The most effective *tool* in answering this very question is research.

## 1.7 | Discussion

1. First list and discuss three to five major takeaways from Sections 1.2 through 1.4 with a small group of peers. In what ways do the concepts of research as a tool and inquiry to improve practice resonate with you?
2. Carefully examine three main school improvement process questions as outlined at the end of Section 1.4. Now, think about these questions from a point of you of your current role (e.g., an educator, education leader, or aspiring administrator) and challenge yourself to answer these three questions—which question(s) did you find most difficult to answer and why?
3. In Section 1.5, you were asked to examine three excerpts from published research studies, which ONE of the three resonated with you most and why?

## 1.8 | Assignment:

### Interactive Exercise: Adverse Childhood Experiences study and Paper Tigers

By using research as a tool, we can use research to build better practice and inform our work as practitioners, education leaders, and school administrators. This exercise gives an explicit example of how research into adverse childhood experiences (ACEs) changed the approach of an Alternative School.

**Step 1:** Review the report posted here https://centerforyouthwellness.org/wp-content/uploads/2020/02/hidden-crisis-errataversion.pdf. This resource is available online and serves as a good example of descriptive and basic data analysis. Read the report and take note of any findings that particularly strike you.

Page 14 of the report states that the "data illustrate, all too clearly, the lifelong consequences of unaddressed adverse experiences in childhood. California must seize this opportunity to promote the health and success of California's children and families by addressing the impact of ACEs." **Are you convinced? Why or why not?**

Appendix A of the report describes the data collection and data analyses. Reread this section looking for phrases or concepts that are unfamiliar to you. **Make a list of those**—this course will strive to answer the most common uncertainties.

Finally, look at the list of ACEs listed on page 17. How would these childhood experiences affect your students? If you are inclined, **take a tally** of your own ACEs. How might this inform how you teach or lead?

**Step 2:** The report from the Center for Youth Wellness depicts the fundamental purpose of data as evidence. Evidence that can be turned into usable information. How can these particular findings inform policy—and then create actionable change?

Paper Tigers is a documentary film that shows an alternative high school in Washington where the principal learned about ACEs and Toxic Stress. As a result of this information, the school changed many of its pedagogical and disciplinary practices. You can see the film trailer here: https://www.youtube.com/watch?v=iV3wzUhJSKs. **What strikes you most about the trailer? Do you see any of your students here? Did the principal make a good decision? Do you think this informed approach had long-term benefits to the students?**

*Note*: This movie is available to rent online if you want to watch the entire movie. Although there is minimal discussion about data, it does tell powerful stories of students and trauma-informed practices.

## References

Hargreaves, A., & Fullan, M. (2012). *Professional capital: Transforming teaching in every school* (1st ed.). Teachers College Press.

Leithwood, K., Seashore-Louis, K., Anderson, S., & Wahlstro, K. (2004). Review of research: How leadership influences student learning. Commissioned by Wallace Foundation: University of Minnesota & University of Toronto.

# CHAPTER 2

# The Basics: Review of Concepts in Research

*Where do I start?*

## 2.1 | Introduction

Before jumping into research designs and methods, we must review few basic concepts. In this chapter, we discuss the importance of making sense of research, being able to read statistical reports, provide an overview of the scientific method, and review basic elements of a research study. After reviewing these basic concepts, we get you started on the path of thinking about your own research through the Plan of Action Part I Assignment. Do note that the Plan of Action Part I, the application assignment, is the first of several assignments included in this textbook designed to engage you in application of learned concepts as you learn them, and encourage you to utilize research as a *tool* in your own school or educational context.

## 2.2 | The Importance of Understanding How to Read Statistics

A critical part of using **data** in Educational Research is understanding the basic elements in statistical results. Yet, students often avoid this information because they have not been introduced to basic statistical literacy. When looking at data, especially analyses, the tables, charts, and statistical markings may be quite off-putting. Even so, it is essential to understand some basic concepts in "reading research"—this is important: the data only becomes *useable* information once it is transformed by analysis.

Educators, education leaders, and administrators have another important reason to understand how to read statistics: they are often trying new interventions in the classroom, or new professional development training for teachers, or designing a counseling session on substance abuse prevention programs for adolescents to minimize dropout rates. These interventions can cost many thousands of dollars, take many months to implement, and usurp untold hours for training and dissemination. If practitioners do not know whether an intervention works, they may try something that has little probability of being successful with many wasted resources. The takeaway point that should be noted, ongoing examination and analysis of data should assist practitioners in making critical decisions.

One of the fundamentals of understanding data is to allow your own curiosity to find the story the data are relaying on. Data and data elements (called variables) are designed to essentially show relationships. When we look at the results, we want to better understand these relationships: *What was expected? Are there inconsistencies? What is the story? Does something look out of place?*

> Data represent a set of *qualitative* and/or *quantitative* facts collected for reference and/or analysis
>
> Primary Data represent firsthand data gathered by the researcher
>
> Secondary Data represent data collected by others (the primary source) and made available for researchers and practitioners to use for their own research and work

As an example, the fictional Santa Bonita Elementary School District reports math proficiency percentages every year for all schools in the district. District leaders were excited to see the large gains made in 2017 as shown in Table 2.1—they did not understand that the large gain should have raised many questions. However, observing gains this large should have caused the district to begin a data analysis process to truly understand the *"why"* behind these gains. Instead, they incorrectly attributed the gains in proficiency to improvements in teaching methods—in reality, however, the state had simply changed the scoring standards for proficiency, elevating scores across the entire state.

**Table 2.1:** Percent Math Proficiency in Elementary Schools

|  | 2014 (%) | 2015 (%) | 2016 (%) | 2017 (%) |
|---|---|---|---|---|
| Sunshine Elementary | 34 | 32 | 36 | 49 |
| Harbor Elementary | 30 | 28 | 29 | 46 |
| Rio Elementary | 37 | 39 | 33 | 52 |

Imagine, if Santa Bonita Elementary School District had invested many thousands of dollars for a math proficiency program in 2015, they might incorrectly attribute those gains to a pricey intervention rather than a recalibrated score. As a nascent education leader and aspiring administrator, it is particularly important to build an understanding of how to read data and understand their meaning. The importance of observing the data and then asking questions is critical to ensure sound decision-making.

> **Activity** With a peer or in a small group, review information presented in Table 2.2. As you review the information, talk aloud through what you are seeing, and then ask questions to discover the relationships shown in the table.

**Table 2.2:** County Report: 2018–2019 Suspension Count by Most Serious Offense Category

| Ethnicity | Cumulative Enrollment | Total Suspensions | Violent Incident (Injury) | Violent Incident (No Injury) | Weapons Possession | Illicit Drug Related | Defiance Only | Other Reasons |
|---|---|---|---|---|---|---|---|---|
| African American | 1,798 | 399 | 32 | 229 | 11 | 29 | 83 | 15 |
| American Indian or Alaska Native | 337 | 25 | 0 | 15 | 0 | 5 | 5 | 0 |
| Asian | 3,257 | 54 | 6 | 30 | 2 | 9 | 3 | 4 |
| Filipino | 299 | 10 | 1 | 6 | 0 | 3 | 0 | 0 |
| Hispanic or Latino | 45,725 | 3,509 | 415 | 1,606 | 126 | 600 | 654 | 108 |
| Pacific Islander | 191 | 19 | 1 | 9 | 1 | 5 | 3 | 0 |
| White | 9,306 | 700 | 82 | 356 | 33 | 85 | 116 | 28 |
| Two or More Races | 822 | 54 | 11 | 27 | 0 | 5 | 8 | 3 |

*(Continued)*

| Ethnicity | Cumulative Enrollment | Total Suspensions | Violent Incident (Injury) | Violent Incident (No Injury) | Weapons Possession | Illicit Drug Related | Defiance Only | Other Reasons |
|---|---|---|---|---|---|---|---|---|
| Not Reported | 329 | 24 | 1 | 14 | 1 | 1 | 5 | 2 |
| **Total** | **62,064** | **4,794** | **549** | **2,292** | **174** | **742** | **877** | **160** |

*Source:* Merced County Report Disaggregated by Ethnicity

Link to URL: Suspension Count Report - Merced County (CA Dept of Education)

At first glance, you might be surprised that these data from California Department of Education (CDE) are parsed into race categories. Why do you think they did? Also, you may wonder how the categories are defined—Which types of incidents are reported as *violent* or *other*? Luckily, the CDE data on the DataQuest website includes a Report Glossary that defines these categories. As you take a close look, one table cell really stands out in terms of cumulative enrollment: More than 45,000 students are categorized as Hispanic/Latino out of just over 62,000 students in the entire county—that is, almost 74% of the county—this seems like an important part of the story.

Another relationship we can examine in this table is that of the number of Violent Incidents with Injuries compared to Total Suspensions. Do any of the Ethnicity categories seem to have a *disproportionate* or outside-the-average number of Violent Incidents with Injuries compared to Total Suspensions? We see that Hispanic have the highest count of suspensions for Violent Incidents with Injuries at 415 for the 2018 to 2019 school year. Further, if you divide the 415 by the total number of suspensions (3,509), you will get 11.83%. Here is another part of the story: Violent Incidents with Injuries make up almost 12% of the reasons Hispanic/Latino students are suspended from school. But is that a disproportionate percentage compared to the county as a whole? If you do the math, you will see that a total of 549 students were suspended for Violent Incidents with Injuries; divided by the total number of suspensions (4,794), you will get 11.45%—which is not that different from the 11.83% for Hispanic/Latino students. For African American students, the percentage is below the county average: 8.02%.

We can see that the relationship of suspensions for Violent Incidents with Injuries, compared to total number of suspensions, is fairly steady. That could be the end of story here, if this proportion is your topic of interest.

However, if you are trying to read further into this "data story," you might notice that there is quite a striking relationship between race and being suspended, period. In fact, more than one of the five students who identify as Black or African American in Merced County were suspended in the 2018 to 2019 school year (Table 2.3). If we were studying disproportionate impact of suspensions on Black students, these data would be an important evidence for our research. If you are an administrator looking at systems that perpetuate inequality in the Merced County schools, these data could be critical when reviewing and ameliorating policies that maintain this disciplinary practice.

**Table 2.3:** 2018–2019 percent of Suspensions by Total Enrollment: Merced County Report, Disaggregated by Ethnicity

| Ethnicity | Cumulative Enrollment | Total Suspensions | Percent |
|---|---|---|---|
| African American | 1,798 | 399 | 22.19 |
| American Indian or Alaska Native | 337 | 25 | 7.42 |
| Asian | 3,257 | 54 | 1.66 |

*(Continued)*

Table 2.3 Flame Temperature of Common Fuels (*Continued*)

| Ethnicity | Cumulative Enrollment | Total Suspensions | Percent |
|---|---|---|---|
| Filipino | 299 | 10 | 3.34 |
| Hispanic or Latino | 45,725 | 3,509 | 7.67 |
| Pacific Islander | 191 | 19 | 9.95 |
| White | 9,306 | 700 | 7.52 |
| Two or More Races | 822 | 54 | 6.57 |
| Not Reported | 329 | 24 | 7.29 |
| **Total** | **62,064** | **4,794** | **7.72** |

## 2.3 | Scientific Method

As we (the authors) have been stressing the importance of thinking of research as a tool, we might consider the offer of the Scientific Method as a series of steps in how to use that tool. The Scientific Method presents a deceptively simple recipe for the phases of knowledge acquisition as an orderly construct. Of course, as can be seen with the Merced County Suspension rates example above, research can be messy. However, the construct of the Scientific Method provides a tautological process for finding evidence—and iteratively building on those findings.

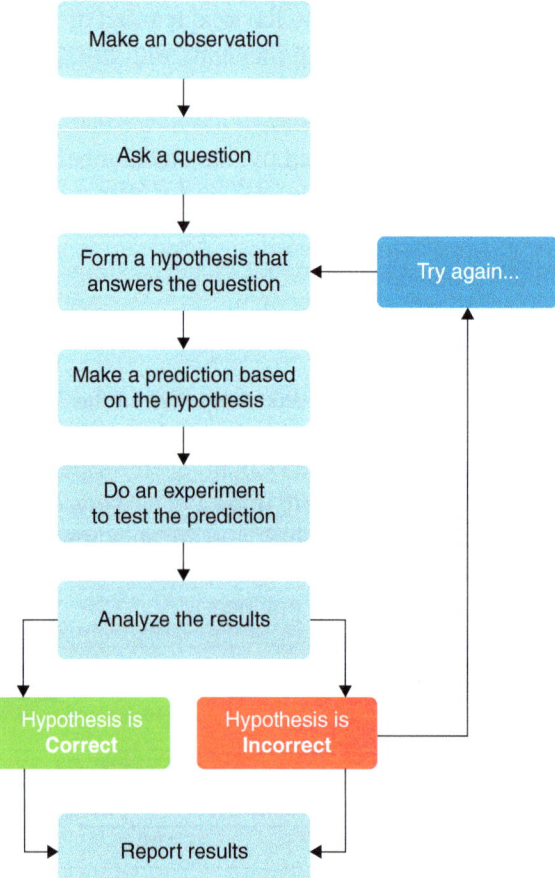

Figure 2.1: Steps Within the Scientific Method

# Chapter 2: The Basics: Review of Concepts in Research

> **Food for thought** What if you were to use the Scientific Method to build a conceptual model regarding the observation of the disproportionate impact of suspensions on black students in Merced County? What would your questions be? What hypothesis might you develop? What "experiment" would you use to test your hypothesis?

The steps in the Scientific Method align directly with the essential elements of research studies; we (the authors) believe it is at the crux of the standardized way we build research studies in every discipline, although it is not always evident.

## Elements of an Education Research Study

As you read research reports and published studies, it is important to know the elements that typically comprise the organization of these works. Although many journals and publishers may vary in what they might title different sections of a paper, the reporting of a study usually includes the following elements.

*The Problem Statement*—Sometimes called an "Introduction." Here, an author names their topic of interest. What is the issue being examined and why is it important? Also included should be very basic description of the issue along with its importance to the field and to the reader.

*Literature Review*—What are the foundational concepts that have contributed to the issue of interest? What is known? What has not been discovered? What are the author's research questions?

*Study Methods*—What design has the author undertaken to better answer the research questions? Which data sources will be used? Will the author undertake their own data collection? What instruments will be used? What are the independent and dependent variables? What is the sample population? What type of analytical method was used? What software was used for the analysis?

*Results*—This section should include a mundane description of the results. The author should not include any inferences or deductions here. Just a simple description of what was found.

*Discussion*—This section is where the author states the meaning of their findings. What the outcomes indicated and the answers to their research questions.

*Conclusion*—This can be thought of as the "Therefore . . . " section. What do the findings indicate? How will these findings have an effect in the field of Education? This section should include limitations of the reported study and areas for future study.

## Topic of Focus and Research Questions

When reading published research studies, you will encounter a research question or a topic of focus. Both serve as a starting point and a blueprint for the research study, so to speak. For example, as a part of your assignment, you are asked to look into an equity issue at your school site—*Where do I start?* you may ask, or you might have other ideas but are unsure how to narrow those down to a research question or problem statement to focus of vision of the research project. The good news is that you are not alone. All researchers and practitioners embarking on a research project are faced with this dilemma in the initial stages of the project. That is, we are interested in examining X but do not know all the Y variables that must be accounted for, which are also required to help shape the research question. *So what do we do?* Simple, we look into data and ask questions. *We ask, "what could be missing from this story?"* We approach stakeholders and those with know-how to acquire more information about our topic. As an example, if you were to investigate an equity issue or equity gap with your school, speaking with the school stakeholders with the know-how, that is, educator colleagues, school leaders, and administrators at the school site will merit much helpful insight into your inquiry and, thus, help narrow down your research question and focus. Now, do not be alarmed if your initial topic will shift (sometimes entirely) after speaking to school stakeholders and those with know-how—this is expected! The more informed and focused your research question/topic is in its initial stages, the better off you will be in a long run.

There are generally two types of research questions: quantitative and qualitative. It is important to consider the type of questions you pose since the type or types of research questions will essentially determine the type of data needed to answer these questions. For example, quantitative questions would deal with numbers, percentages, and statistics (including descriptive statistics discussed later in this chapter). Qualitative questions, on the other hand, are designed to inquire about lived or professional insights, observations and opinions, as well as derive the meaning from stakeholders by understanding their experiences and stories. Below, we provide examples of quantitative and qualitative research questions that are generally addressing a similar topic, but would require different types of data to answer.

QUANTITATIVE: What is the average student academic performance on mathematics for Urban Valley Middle School by grade and subgroup as reflected in the state's standardized test for the past three years? Note that this question deals with subgroup and numbers and, therefore, quantitative by nature.

QUALITATIVE: What are the contributing factors that perpetuate the achievement gap in mathematics between English language learners and their English-only counterparts at Urban Valley Middle School?

## Hypothesis

Although we are likely all familiar with the word *hypothesis*, it has a particular meaning in research. Essentially, it is a statement that tries to assert the outcome of a data point of interest. For example, students who receive abstinence-only education during high school will have reduced rates of teenage pregnancy. There can only be two types of hypotheses in a research study: one, there is no difference between two groups (also known as Null Hypothesis) or that there is a difference (the Alternative Hypothesis).

Every research outcome is essentially testing the probability that either the Null or the Alternative hypothesis is true. It is the resulting probability that determines whether a finding has statistical significance (Fisher, 1956). Now that you know the basic purpose of a hypothesis in a research application, *when do I use a hypothesis?* you may ask. A hypothesis is appropriate when you want to test how two variables (items/things/groups) relate to one another. In other words, you hypothesize that there is a relationship between X and Y (Alternative) or there is no relationship between X and Y (Null).

For example, as an equity-driven leader and aspiring administrator who wants to bring their education community together in authentic and all-encompassing ways, you have a "theory" that establishing parental affinity groups outside of school hours will increase parental participation in school-related activities. Therefore, you theorize or hypothesize that

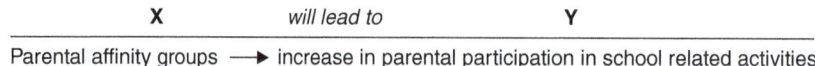

| **X** | *will lead to* | **Y** |
|---|---|---|
| Parental affinity groups | → | increase in parental participation in school related activities |

**Figure 2.2:** Conceptual Model: Understanding Hypothesis

## Sampling

Now that we discussed few basics, it is important to understand that researchers usually need a sample from their population, let us discuss some methods most salient to the field of education.

Most of you are familiar with a census; of course, we mostly think of the census that occurs every 10 years in the United States and many other countries have their own intervals of population counting. The greatest advantage of a census is that you do not need to apply any statistical analysis to get a true count. You have found the "truth" by counting every single member of the population. Table 2.4 demonstrates actual numbers; no estimates are needed. However, because a census counts every person in the population, it can get very expensive. In fact, the cost of the 2020 U.S. Census is expected to exceed $15 billion (https://www.gao.gov/highrisk/decennial-census).

**Table 2.4:** High School Attainment of the U.S. Population Aged 25 and Older by Selected Population Characteristics (in Thousands)

| Population Characteristic | Total | Percent | Number |
|---|---|---|---|
| Population 25 and older | 212,132 | 88 | 186,676 |
| **Age** | | | |
| 25 to 34 | 43,006 | 91 | 38,920 |
| 35 to 44 | 39,919 | 89 | 35,408 |
| 45 to 64 | 83,213 | 89 | 74,392 |
| 65 and older | 45,994 | 84 | 38,773 |
| **Sex** | | | |
| Male | 101,888 | 88 | 89,661 |
| Female | 110,245 | 89 | 97,898 |
| **Race and Hispanic Origin** | | | |
| White alone | 168,420 | 89 | 149,557 |
| Non-Hispanic White alone | 140,638 | 93 | 130,793 |
| Black alone | 25,420 | 87 | 22,115 |
| Asian alone | 12,331 | 89 | 10,987 |
| Hispanic (of any race) | 31,020 | 67 | 20,690 |
| **Nativity Status** | | | |
| Native born | 175,519 | 92 | 161,126 |
| Foreign born | 36,613 | 72 | 26,361 |
| **Disability Status** | | | |
| With a disability | 28,052 | 79 | 22,049 |
| Without a disability | 183,351 | 90 | 164,833 |

*Source:* U.S. Census Bureau, 2015 (Ryan & Bauman, 2016).

Of course, researchers rarely have a $15 billion budget for their own studies. That is, when we can employ a method called "sampling," we use a sample to estimate the correct counts. For example, the Youth Risk Behavior Surveillance System (YRBSS) was begun by the Centers for Disease Control and Prevention (CDC) in 1991 to provide educators, public health providers, researchers, and policy makers to monitor the trends in health risks for adolescents. Because collecting data from all students across the country or in a state would be tremendously costly, researchers designed a complex sampling strategy to collect data from fewer respondents but would be representative of the general population. Essentially, they first selected a few school—sites and then randomly selected active classes in those schools during a required period to administer the survey to students attending those classes (Prevention, 2013).

Ultimately, although the costs are greatly reduced, the design creates a much more complex implementation methodology and introduces probable error in the results. Therefore, the data analyses become quite complex. Certainly, each approach—whether a census or a sample—comes with its own complexities and costs. One thing to keep in mind is that we get statistics only from sampled studies—from census studies, we get population parameters (in other words, statistics only exist when we are estimating the "truth").

## Descriptive Statistics

In very basic terms, statistics are the quantitative representations of the elements and outcomes of a study. Every journal article includes descriptive statistics—these descriptions are an important part of summarizing data. Certainly, you are already familiar with many of these descriptive statistics. If they involve only one variable (i.e., data element), they are called "univariate" and can be displayed in many ways. See link for an example below. When taking a closer look at each row, you will get a good sense of the students involved in the presented study. We then can make the following determinations by looking at this simple descriptive table. See example at the link below:

From: https://benthamopen.com/contents/pdf/TOEDUJ/TOEDUJ-6-18.pdf

Susan, D. G.,* Alan, C. C, Andreas, W. S., & William, R. (2013). Bentham Open Access The Effect of demographic variables upon university students' service learning experiences in marketing. *The Open Education Journal, 2013, 6,* 18–24. 1874-9208/13 2013.

1. There is a fairly equal distribution of males and females.
2. Well over half of the sample was between the ages of 21 and 25.
3. Most students were White, but there is some distribution of other races.
4. Which major was mostly represented in this sample?

Descriptive statistics can involve a multitude of display options—many of you have seen pie charts, histograms, bar graphs, and more complex depictions of sample data. Because research is interested in discovering and validating relationships, looking at descriptive statistics gives you a better feel for the possible relationships that will be unearthed. Not only does this help in understanding the research subjects, but it can help in evaluating the validity of a study. What if the table above had 78% males? Or 2% Latino? It would certainly inform your opinions about what kind of findings could be determined when a sample is skewed.

Of course, many people look at charts, tables, and figures every day that describe the data collected in a study. The following graphic (Figure 2.3) displays an enjoyable and eye-catching way of depicting data.

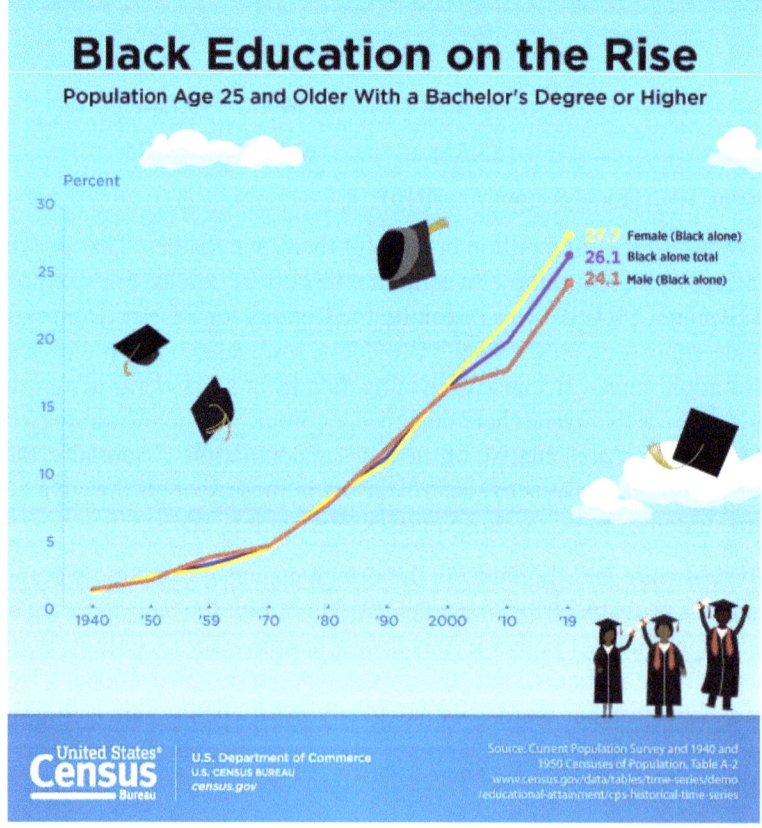

**Figure 2.3:** US Census: Black Education on the Rise
*Source:* CDC.

One important tidbit to remember is that descriptive statistics describe the findings, they do not make any conclusions about the ultimate findings. When we do want to state our interpretations of findings, researchers often utilize inferential statistics. When researchers discuss inferential statistics, they are referring to generalizing results from the sample to the larger population. There are a multitude of techniques—from basic to ultra-complicated by which researchers create these inferences. What is important is to differentiate descriptive (which describes only the sample) from inferential (which attempts to describe the general population).

## 2.4 | Application: *Where Do I Start?*

Application of learning is how one solidifies their knowledge. In this section, we introduce you to several components or steps to get you thinking about your research interests as you narrow these interests down to a manageable topic leading to first a topic, then a research question—yes, multiple steps just to get to the topic and research question! What we want you to know is that any research project is a process and not a *TASK*. Hence, as you get started on the path of conducting research and using research as *a tool*, be mindful of the process, since one of the main elements in research is the process itself (see the unpacking of the scientific method above), which often requires contemplation, investigation, and at times (and those times are often) reconsideration.

### Education Indicators and Standards

Since all states in the United States regard access to K-12 education as constitutional obligation as part of state constitution, each state in the union has specific indicators, learning standards, and goals as these relate to student academic performance and well-being for their public school districts. Having the knowledge about these and, more importantly, knowing how to access this information, is a place to start.

For the purposes of unpacking this initial step and engaging you in a practical example, we will use California's model as an example since CDE supports multiple, publicly available databases and publishes annual data on many parameters that align with the state's indicators of focus for public schools and districts. These indicators are used to collect data from the state's public school districts by means of the California Longitudinal Pupil Achievement Data System (CALPADS) and from the testing vendors responsible for standardized test assessment data. As of this writing, California's six indicators were as follows:

1. Academic Indicator (reported separately for English language arts/literacy [ELA] and mathematics assessments)
2. English Learner Progress
3. Chronic Absenteeism
4. Graduation Rate
5. Suspension Rate
6. College/Career Readiness (includes Grade 11 assessment results)

California Department of Education (2021): https://www.cde.ca.gov/ta/ac/cm/sicadashboardfaq.asp

Although these indicators may appear to be self-explanatory, it is important to know how they are defined and applied. Therefore, we provide a brief overview for each below.

**The Academic Indicator** deals with student academic achievement on standardized tests. These achievement data are reported by population; therefore, it is important to examine these data with a specific population in mind.

Next, is the **English Learn Progress Indicator**, which encompasses not only the progress toward proficiency in the English language or as evidenced by English Language Proficiency Assessments for

California (ELPAC), but also classification and reclassification district criteria out of the English learner status that typically varies from district to district and at times, significantly. It is important to note that the two, that is, proficiency in the English language and district reclassification criteria, are often not one and the same. Therefore, reclassification rates, in particular, could be more dependent upon a district's reclassification criteria than a student's measured proficiency in the English language (Okhremtchouk et al., 2016).

**Chronic Absenteeism** is focused on documenting the patterns of students who are chronically absent. Specifically, the focus of Chronic Absenteeism indicator is on the students who were absent or missed school for 10 or more percent of an academic year for any reason—that is, these include unexcused and excused absences, as well as any other absences due to suspensions, transition time when changing schools, among other reasons. Therefore, let us say out of a 180-day school year, a student who is absent for 18 or more days will fall into the category of being chronically absent.

Forth indicator is **Graduation Rate**, which encompasses a combined four- and five-year graduation rate and is based on the number of students who graduate with a regular high school diploma in either four or five years. This indicator only applies and reported for districts and school that include grades nine through 12.

The next indicator is **Suspension Rate**, which is based on the number of students who have been suspended at least once in a given academic year. It should be noted that for those students who are suspended more than once, they are only counted once under this indicator—recurrent suspensions are not accounted for.

Finally, the **College and Career Readiness** indicator measures how school districts and schools prepare their students for success after graduation. Graduates who are classified as "prepared" must meet at least one of the eight criteria to be classified as prepared.

As you review the above-listed indicators and their definitions, start thinking about these in the contexts of the school where you work or, alternatively, your neighborhood school that you are well familiar with. Select one indicator to examine further. Please remember that this is a process and your selection of the school site could change later. At this initial juncture, we want you to have a school site in mind in the context of one of the indicators listed above. Upon selecting an indicator, choose one of the publicly available databases from the list provided in Table 2.5. Once there, go through the steps of selecting the county, district, and school and find data for your selected indicator.

**Table 2.5:** California Department of Education Data Sources

| Source (CDE) | Link to Website |
|---|---|
| EdData | https://www.ed-data.org/ |
| DataQuest | https://dq.cde.ca.gov/dataquest/ |
| California School Dashboard | https://www.caschooldashboard.org/ |
| Local Control and Accountability Plan (LCAP): | https://www.cde.ca.gov/re/lc/ |
| School Accountability Report Card (SARC): | https://www.cde.ca.gov/ta/ac/sa/ |

> **Food for thought** Now that you began to examine student data in a context of a school site and chosen indicator, what stands out to you? Are these data what you had expected? Why or why not? Start thinking about potential equity gaps as you parallel these data with the school's context and perhaps education community dynamics—What might be the contributing factors that allow for some of the achievement gaps to persist? Documents your thoughts and discuss with peers.

## 2.5 | Conclusion

In this chapter, we covered the basic concepts to help you make sense of research, how to read research, and how to think about your own research. This chapter is one of the first foundational chapters designed to unpack the first steps in the process of thinking about a research study, no matter how small or large. Likewise, as we discuss these concepts, our aim is to engage you in practical application of knowledge to bring the theoretical concepts to life in light of a school site context. The application section (Section 2.4) of this chapter provides an important entryway to thinking about data constructively, knowing how to find data, and begin searching for data. Likewise, the two subsequent sections are designed to engage you in critical thinking by means of discussion (Section 2.6) and supply a template so you can begin formulating your own research (Section 2.7). The Plan of Action Part I template under the assignment section intended to help you document as well as continue to think about your topic and, ultimately, shape your research question. This is the first of several assignments in this textbook designed to build on your acquired knowledge one step at a time in the end leading to either (a) a longitudinal documentation (over a three-year course) and analysis of school site data around an existing equity gap paving the foundation for creating a plan for evidenced-based strategies to make change possible or (b) a research proposal for a larger study. This step-by-step process is intestinally designed to encourage you to think about and utilize research as a *tool* in your professional and educational context. As we move forward to the next chapter, we invite you to think about this text and each exercise engagement as a process consisting of steps that require circling back, rethinking, revisiting, and adjustments as you learn more and expand your knowledge whether through an examination of academic literature (Chapter 3) or by taking a more in-depth look into existing data (Chapter 4). Research is a journey with infinite destination and brief stops along the way.

## 2.6 | Discussion

1. As you reflect on the concepts discussed in Sections 2.2 and 2.3, what are the dangers of education research? Can you think of examples where research can be misunderstood or even abused? How can education research add to lifting equity and inclusion?
2. When reflecting on practical application of knowledge (Section 2.4), what stood out to you most? In what way or ways working with data directly help you gain a deeper perspective of the school site?
3. As you reflect on the Black Education on the rise graphic (Section 2.3, Figure 2.3), what research questions could you think of to dig deeper into this data source? What data/information was missing?
4. When analyzing the six sate indicators from the CALPADS system (Section 2.4), are there one or two of the indicators that stand out as the most used by public school institutions? As you answer this question, from your perspective, are there one or two that appear to be the most abused and in what way(s)?

## 2.7 | Assignment: Plan of Action Part I—A starting Point

Now that you engaged in a search for school site data, it is time for you to start thinking about the topic and research question that you might want to explore further. Because this textbook is designed to provide tools for educators, educator leaders, and aspiring administrators to use research as a tool to improve the field of education, we suggest that you frame your topic/question as an issue of equity that the school site is yet to address or struggles with. As we guide you through this process, we will circle back to the equity issue often throughout exercises included in this text. To start you on the path of documenting your thoughts, identifying your topic/research questions, we provided a template to help you get started—the Plan of Action Part I. The Plan of Action is designed to serve as a starting point to help you think about an inquiry on the topic aligned with your interest and grounded in one of the state indicators.

---

### Template: Plan of Action Part I

[Please delete all directions prior to submitting your Plan of Action assignment]

## Instructions

Plan of Action Part I template provides a starting point and sets the direction for engaging in research and using research as a tool. This assignment is one of the first building blocks and is expected to be revisited and modified as you continue to engage and conceptualize your project.

The following components are to be included in this assignment:

- State Indicator
- Population of Focus
- **Topic**
- **Overarching Question**
  - **Specific Research Questions** *(as applicable)*

## State Indicator

Your first step is to select one from the six indicators listed in Section 2.4. Your selection must be in the context of a school site that you are well familiar with. We suggest that you select the school where you work, intern, or volunteer.

## Population of Focus

After examining data per your chosen indicator, select a student subgroup or several that triggered your interest. Please remember that your select might change as you continue to engage with data.

## Topic

Start thinking about and determine a research topic—it is okay if you are unsure! But, you have to start somewhere—remember, you can revise your topic later. While considering a topic, be sure to draw on your professional experiences and areas of interest as well as the application of knowledge exercise in Section 2.4. HINT: You may want to explore several California Department of Education databases sites included in Section 2.4 before settling on a topic to see what data are available—this further exploration will also assist with population selection

## Overarching Question

The overarching question should serve as an umbrella for the issue/topic you are investigating. The question should broadly address/encompass the aim of your specific research questions (to be constructed below). Additionally, this question will guide you in your searches for literature (Chapter 3) and will help to sustain focus.

> **Research Questions**
>
> Unlike your overarching question, your research questions should be precise and specific. While conceptualizing and constructing your research questions, make sure that they do not lead to a yes/no answer. Hence, starters such as how, to what degree, why, and so on, are helpful in thinking about your questions and your topic of interest. HINT: Consult Section 2.3.
>
> 1. _____
>
> 2. _____
>
> 3. _____

# References

CA Dept of Education. (2018–2019). *2018–19 Suspension count by most serious offense category, merced county report, disaggregated by ethnicity.* https://dq.cde.ca.gov/dataquest/dqCensus/DisSuspCount.aspx?cds=24&agglevel=County&year=2018-19

California Department of Education. (2020, December). *Dashboard State Indicators FAQs. California School Dashboard and System of Support.* https://www.cde.ca.gov/ta/ac/cm/sicadashboardfaq.asp

Fisher, R. (1956). *Statistical methods and scientific inference.* Hafner Publishing CO.

Geringer, S. D., Canton, A. C., Stratemeyer, A. W., & Rice, W. (2013, November 11). The effect of demographic variables upon university students' service–learning experiences in marketing. *The Open Education Journal, 6,* 18–24. https://doi.org/:10.2174/1874920801306010018

Prevention, C. F. (2013). Methodology of the youth risk behavior surveillance system—2013. *Morbidity and Mortality Weekly Report, 62(1),* 20. https://www.cdc.gov/mmwr/pdf/rr/rr6201.pdf

Okhremtchouk, I. S., Archibeque, R., Clark, A., Baca, E. C., & Sellu, G. S. (2016). *Sentenced for life: An analysis of district reclassification criteria for English language learners in California.* Paper presented at American Education Research Association (AERA), Washington, DC.

Ryan, C. L., & Bauman, K. (2016). *Educational attainment in the United States: 2015.* U.S. Census Bureau. https://www.census.gov/content/dam/Census/library/publications/2016/demo/p20-578.pdf

U.S. Census Bureau. (2021, January 13). Black education on the rise. *Census.gov.* https://www.census.gov/library/visualizations/2021/comm/black-education.html

# CHAPTER 3

# The Stepping Stones of Data-informed Practice: Academic Literature Search, Literature Review & Annotated Bibliography

*Now that I have a topic, where do I look?*

## 3.1 | Introduction

The purpose of this chapter is to continue to build on the foundational concepts discussed in Chapter 2. Both chapters (Chapters 2 and 3) are designed to convey the first steps in conceptualizing and envisioning your future research project. Previously, we asked you to think about the state's indicators (using California's indicators as an example) and select one that best aligns with your interests. We also asked you to choose a familiar school (either where you work or live). Then, with the help of the Plan of Action Part I assignment, we asked you to think about a potential topic and start drafting an overarching research question and two to three specific/adjacent questions. The next step is to explore academic literature and empirical research on your chosen topic.

This chapter takes you through various essential steps as you begin your literature search to expand your knowledge on the topic of your choice. We also cover the use of an annotated bibliography as a steppingstone for constructing a literature review and unpack the importance of juxtaposition in a literature review. Lastly, we engage you in an application of knowledge exercise and ask you to participate in human subjects training to make you IRB eligible to conduct research.

## 3.2 | Making Sense of the Field

Knowing what the field has to say about your chosen topic is a must-have step in the process of using research as a *tool*. That is, you want to expand your knowledge and learn along the way what research studies and reports have to say about the topic you selected. In other words, you want to make sense of the field pertaining to your topic and deepen your knowledge along the way.

For the purposes of an example, let us assume that as part of the exercise in Chapter 2, you selected "Academic Performance" as your indicator of focus and after initial review of data concerning student achievement on standardized tests, you noticed that there is a significant performance gap between English language learners and their English-only counterparts in mathematics. Therefore, your Plan of Action Part I might include information as outlined below:

| | |
|---|---|
| **Indicator:** | Academic Performance |
| **Topic:** | Academic Performance in Mathematics |
| **Population of focus:** | English language learners as compared to their English-only counterparts |

> **Overarching Research Question:** Given the academic performance gap in mathematics between English language learners and their English-only counterparts, what are the contributing factors affecting this achievement equity gap at the school site?

You want to use this information to be more efficient and, therefore, effective in your search of what the field has to say about your chosen topic. Notice that in the example above, the indicator, topic, and population of focus are aligned. There is a logical connection between the three and the three serve as building blocks for one another. These building blocks are paramount in constructing the overarching research question, which must reflect all three elements, that is, indicator, topic, the population of focus. Likewise, the overarching research question must frame the examination to come.

In the example above, the overarching question proposes to look into the contributing factors that affect the achievement gap and, therefore, create the academic performance equity gap between English language learners and their English-only counterparts. Clearly identifying the topic, population of focus, and connecting these dots while centering the research question will not only help focus your study, but will also focus your literature search.

> **Exercise:** Find a peer with similar interests and swap your Plan of Action Part I assignments from Chapter 2. Then review indicator, topic, the population of focus, as well as overarching and focused research questions for alignment. As you review your peer's work, engage in discussions about chosen topics, research question(s), and provide feedback.

## Peer-review and Peer Collaboration

Before we unpack the literature search process and steps, we would like to take a minute to discuss peer-review and peer collaboration. Empirical research studies are not designed, done, or vetted in isolation. Aside from the dependence on collaboration and stakeholder input while doing research, academic journals take between six months and a year or more to evaluate research article submissions. These evaluations of academic work are done through expert double-blind peer-reviews, peer feedback, and at times extensive revisions before manuscripts are accepted for publication. As such, peer review, peer feedback, expert opinion, and stakeholder input all are critical when conducting research. We, researchers, lean heavily on our peers and their expertise, especially, when we get stuck or need to revisit our topics, the focus of our study, or research questions to ensure a more fitted direction. As you continue to read this chapter and before engaging in a literature search, we suggest that you connect with your peers over similar topics of interest and partner with one or several. This connection will allow peer collaboration and afford peer feedback, which will provide support along the way as you dive deeper into your topic and mirror what researchers do as they work through their research projects—rely on their peers for feedback and input!

> **Form Peer-review groups:** Your peer-review group should be limited to two or three people to ensure that the level of review and feedback is fruitful. As you form your peer-review groups, you want to connect over the common interests/topics so you can engage authentically and provide support to one another.

## Recognizing Various Types of Literature

In this section, we discuss the type of literature that you will come across in your search and how to recognize it. In general, there are four different article types. One type is the articles meant to be read by scholars, students studying the subject, and professionals in the field. These types of articles are heavily vetted and peer-reviewed. The second type, such as trade journals or professional journals, is geared towards professionals and practitioners. These articles are meant to relay the most up-to-date information that could be easily translated into practice and considered for implementation. Then there is a type or an area we call "gray literature," which comprises conference papers, research reports (some are preliminary), blogs, and so on. Gray literature is usually designed to provide the most up-to-date information to scholars/researchers, students, professionals, practitioners, and the general public. Additionally, gray literature usually appears without the rigorous peer-review vetting process we spoke of in the prior section. The sharing of these works is designed to stimulate a discussion to allow researchers to connect with peer experts and stakeholders to acquire feedback. And, lastly, popular literature/articles that you might read in newspapers or magazines. Popular literature is designed to be published for the lay public and written so that one would not need to be an expert to make sense of the concepts.

These four types of articles come with a distinct identity that is unique for each type (see Table 3.1). Research literature communicates the findings of original research where the topic and research questions are clearly stated, research methods are identified and spoken about, a review of literature is included to explain how the research at hand extends or builds upon prior empirical studies, and author(s) credentials are listed. On the other hand, the sole purpose of professional literature is to address workplace implementations. Although it is common for professional literature to speak about best practices, the literature review and citations of scholarly works are limited and typically not a central component of a research study. Gray literature is unpublished literature that is often yet to undergo a peer-review process (or, may never). Depending on the type of gray literature (e.g., a research study presented at a conference vs. an opinion essay), it may or may not contain an extensive literature review and references list. Finally, popular literature is easy to recognize, and it is also easy to read. Popular literature is written or reported by reporters, not scholars. You will notice minimal citations included in the text, and if expert opinion is offered, it is documented in the form of quote from an interview.

**Table 3.1:** Identifying Article Types (NOTE: give credit to librarian)

| Article Types | How to recognize |
| --- | --- |
| Scholarly/Research Articles | Original research, identified research method, citations, list of references, peer-reviewed and aligned with journal requirements and scope, author credentials are provided |
| Professional Literature | Written to address workplace implementations, limited in-text citations, limited list of references, the review type is aligned with journal requirements and scope and articles may not be subject to rigorous peer-review, author credentials are listed |
| Gray Literature | Unpublished literature including conference papers, government reports, opinion essays, may contain extensive in-text citations and list of references |
| Popular Literature | Easy to read, few or no citations, reporter is the author, and no author credentials listed |

## 3.3 | Literature Search

You are ready to embark on your literature search, now that we have covered the importance of carefully focusing your research by aligning your topic and research question, peer-review and collaboration, as well as being able to recognize and differentiate between types of literature. As you engage in your literature search, you want to use both the topic and population of focus as your "search terms" for several reasons.

> One, it is not uncommon to find that research literature is limited on your chosen topic in conjunction with your population of focus; therefore, you might need to report on the topic and population of focus as it relates to your topic separately to help understand what the field has to say about your topic.

Two, expanding your knowledge about your population of focus even outside of the topic would merit many fruitful benefits. That is, the better you know the population you are about to study, the more contributing variables you can identify. It is important to note that subgroups (be it students or adults) are not monolithic, although data records and databases can present them as such. To this end, it is common for subgroups to be grouped together as sharing heritage or racial backgrounds but be quite unique with respect to home languages spoken, special needs, gender identity, sexual orientation, socioeconomic status among other diverse identities and needs individuals bring into a classroom, school, and other spaces. Therefore, knowing more about your population of focus, will not only expand your understanding about the population you are about to research, but will give you a more in-depth insight that will help inform and shape your study.

Three, having both, a broader understanding of your topic and population of focus, in conjunction and/or separately will help you further shape the research question and, ultimately, the direction of your research.

There are a number of places where you can search for academic literature on your chosen topic and population of focus and most will simply require a computer and internet connection. As a part of your training at a higher education institution, you will likely have access to a library database. The access to literature has improved significantly over the last decade or so and now, even printed text could be scanned and shared electronically by most higher education institutions. Another way to find published research and scholarly literature is through open access academic journals. And, of course, at times it is very rewarding to conduct your search in person at your local or academic library. No matter the method you choose to conduct your search, below we outline steps to get you started.

## Exploring an Institutional Library Database

Most, if not all post-secondary institutions (colleges and universities) subscribe to academic journal archives and provide access through their online system. As an enrolled student, you are able to access these literature sources. Additionally, the online cataloging will likely include a list of available printed resources through your academic library that could be scanned and provided electronically by means of a service ticket filed online. Below, we outline several general basic steps to access your library resources.

1. Find out how and access your institution's library online
2. Learn about in-person and online library "help hours" and learn about the process for "book borrowing" just in case you will need to borrow books
3. Acquire your global campus login to access library database off campus and make sure it works! (*this is essential since knowing how to operate an online database will give you much flexibility*)
4. Once you are in the system, explore and search library databases for scholarly articles and books (see section Search Tips below)

## Open Access Journals: Going Directly to the Source

In the past several decades there has been a strong move toward Open Access Journals to communicate research more quickly and efficiently to practitioners. This move has helped fill a prior gap between the research world and that of the academy, where research and studied best practices were not translating quickly enough to the field of practice and application. Additionally, there was a steep emergence of the scholarly journals purposefully engaging in publishing research by practitioners. All of which, has helped expedite the process for user-informed research based and data-informed practices. Below we provide a list of peer-reviewed journals that do not limit access to readers and are open access:

## Chapter 3: The Stepping Stones of Data-informed Practice

1. *The Journal of Teacher Action Research*: http://www.practicalteacherresearch.com
2. *Journal of School Administration Research and Development:* https://www.ojed.org/index.php/JSARD
3. *Education Policy Analysis Archives*: https://epaa.asu.edu/ojs/index.php/epaa
4. *American Education Research Association (AERA) Open:* https://journals.sagepub.com/home/ero
5. *The Elementary School Journal:* https://www.journals.uchicago.edu/toc/esj/current
6. *The Future of Children* (early childhood education): https://futureofchildren.princeton.edu/publications
7. *Current Issues in Education*: https://cie.asu.edu/ojs/index.php/cieatasu
8. *The Journal of Educational Research*: https://www.tandfonline.com/toc/vjer20/current

## Other Collections and Ways to Search

ERIC database, which is supported by the Institute of Education Science, is a valuable resource to search for scholarly literature. The database includes an option to include full text in your search, which will provide an easy access to academic literature. Additionally, the database provides advanced options to limit your search with a more defined search based on your chosen topic and population of focus. Below we provide a link to the site, directions to acquire full text, and an image of the search done on ERIC to get you started if you choose to explore ERIC as you search for literature. to find literature.

1. Access ERIC database: https://eric.ed.gov/
2. Enter your topic and population of focus in the search field
3. Select other parameters such as, publication date, descriptor and source on the left-hand side, as well as we suggest that you select the peer reviewed option and check the box for full text so you will have access to the full text as an option of your search (see Figure 3.1 for example)

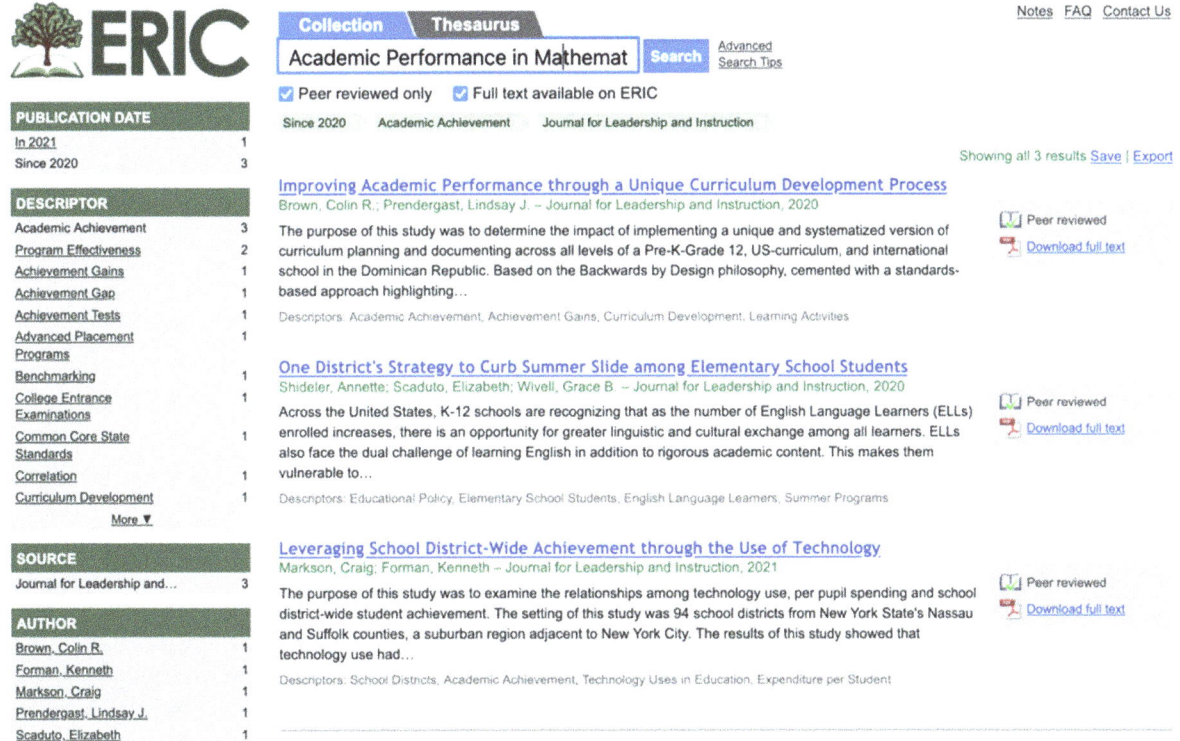

**Figure 3.1:** Example of Search Using ERIC

In the example above, we entered a topic and population of focus from an earlier example: Academic Performance in Mathematics and English language learners. Because we wanted to search original/empirical studies that are fairly recent (since 2020) with "Academic Achievement" as a descriptor we selected those items as well—you will notice that all selections are listed under the search field. Lastly, since we are interested in leadership, we selected *Journal for Leadership and Instruction* as our source. This search merited three articles with full texts, the first two happen to align with our topic and population of focus, as well as (as a bonus) these works studies best practices.

Who does not love a good Google search? Well, with Google Scholar, you are in luck! Google Scholar is another way to search for scholarly literature. Below we provide a link to Google Scholar and an image of our search to serve as an example.

1. Access Google Scholar: https://scholar.google.com
2. Enter your topic and population of focus in the search field
3. Select other parameters on the left-hand side (See Figure 3.2)
4. Screen results and adjust as needed, then repeat the search until you find articles that fit your topic/relevant to your research question(s)

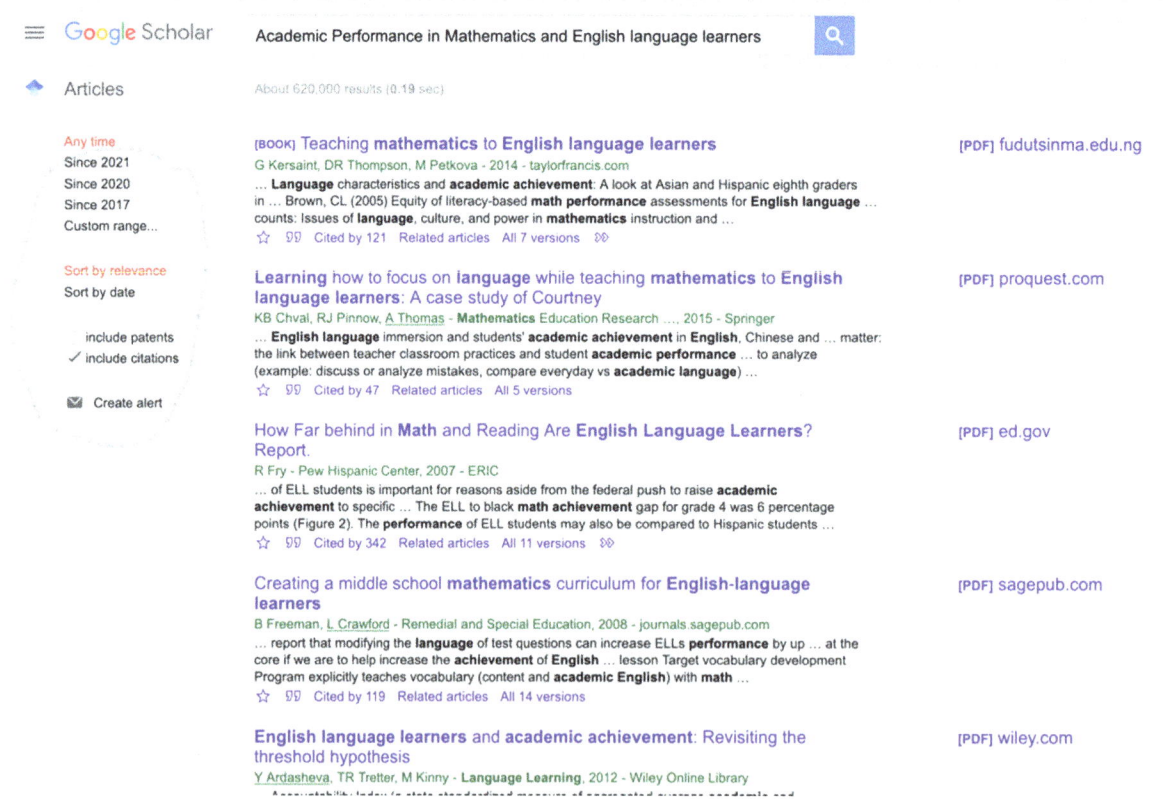

**Figure 3.2:** Google Scholar Search Example

Similar to the prior example, the image depicted in Figure 3.2 lists abundance of search results indicating the availability of full texts (PDF) on the right-hand side. Parameters for the search are selected on the left-hand side where you can search by date of publication and/or relevance. Lastly, you can create a profile on Google Scholar and affiliate your university/institution (see Figure 3.3). By creating a profile and affiliating your institution in Google Scholar, you will automatically receive access to articles and journals that your institution supports/subscribes to. This connected access through Google Scholar is a game-changer for students; finding scholarly work has never been so accessible.

# Chapter 3: The Stepping Stones of Data-informed Practice

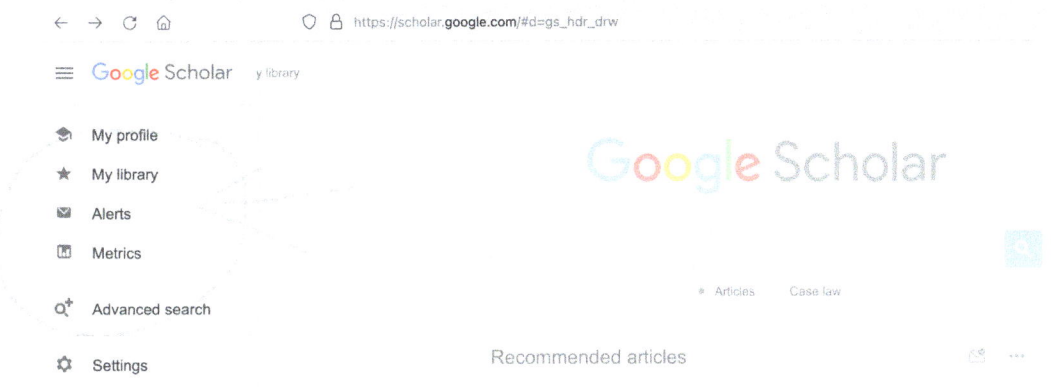

**Figure 3.3:** Create Google Scholar Profile

## Search Tips

As shown in the images above, based on the set parameters, you can end up with few articles or several thousand. And, although, it is usually good to have more options, in the case of research article searches, more is not always better. Therefore, in this section, we outline several tips on how to limit your search and align it more with your chosen topic and population of focus.

**TIP 1:** Draft several search term possibilities in addition to your topic and population of focus that reflect some specific nuances before you begin your search and use these search terms with similar or related meaning by introducing parenthesis (ranging from the narrow to the broad)
   **Examples:**
   - Middle school mathematics AND English language learners
   - Academic performance in mathematics AND (English language learner OR Latino students)

**TIP 2:** Use conjunctions to help with your search. Once you have a list of search terms, link these terms with **"AND" to narrow** your search or use **"OR" to expand** your search.
   **Example:**
   School leadership AND (English learners OR Latino students)

**TIP 3:** If you want the terms to be included exactly when results are generated, use quotation marks around the terms you want to be included.
   **Example:** "English learners" AND "mathematics" AND (school leadership OR administration)

> **Exercise** First, draft a list of terms (see TIP 1). Then review the following website about Boolean operators: https://libguides.mit.edu/c.php?g=175963&p=1158594 to expand upon your knowledge. After engage in a search for literature by using any of the means listed above, for example, going directly to the open access journals, using Google Scholar, ERIC, or your institution's online library—we advise that you try several, if not all! Find anywhere between three to ten scholarly articles and save them for future use.

## Tools to Organize Your Search

Now that you found all this great literature and empirical studies, what are some of the ways to manage all the articles you found? Below we provide a table (Table 3.2) with links to the websites that are designed to assist with organization of articles (PDFs), help with citations, and annotated bibliographies.

Table 3.2: Tools and Resources for Organizing Literature Searches

| Website | URL | Purpose and Use |
|---|---|---|
| **Zotero** | http://www.zotero.org/ | Bibliographic Management:<br>• Save and organize citations, PDFs, links, notes, and more to central location<br>• Drag and drop citations into word and other documents<br>• Export bibliographies<br>• Word-processing and citation integration |
| **Mendeley** | http://www.mendeley.com/ | Reference Manager and PDF Organizer:<br>• Save and organize citations, PDFs, links, notes, and more to central location<br>• Drag and drop citations into word and other documents<br>• Export bibliographies<br>• Word-processing and citation integration |
| **Bibme** | http://www.bibme.org/ | Citation/bibliography generator: APA, MLA, among others. |
| **Citation Machine** | http://citationmachine.net | • Citation/bibliography generator: APA, MLA, among others. |

## 3.4 | A Literature Review: An Art of Juxtaposition

No matter how extensive or brief a literature review is, it should include both a discussion and summary of published literature on a specific topic and/or research question. The general aim of a literature review is to comprehensively and objectively describe extant research (preferably peer-reviewed and of empirical nature), as well as other scholarly works to inform the field and/or make an argument for one's forthcoming study/research project.

Specifically, literature reviews are constructed for several reasons.

> One, some literature reviews are constructed *for descriptive purposes* and are designed to stand on their own to provide a comprehensive overview on a topic to inform practitioners or academic circles by enhancing their knowledge through a comprehensive, up-to-date review of the literature and/or by supporting better decision-making in practice.

> Two, literature reviews are constructed *to make a case* for a study by carefully, comprehensively, and systematically identifying what is in the literature and what is not, that is, what gaps need to be filled, and how a proposed study would aim to fill these gaps. Hence, literature reviews establish a case and need for a research study.

> Three, on a smaller scale, literature reviews are constructed *for investigative purposes*. That is, to carefully investigate what has been established by the field through empirical work/research to inform an idea, a topic, or research question. This reason would apply to many of you (if not all) at this juncture and as you continue to think through and conceptualize your topics and research questions.

*So how do I write a good literature review?*—you may ask. When the three of us discuss literature reviews or good literature reviews, our discussions conclude with the importance of juxtaposition. That is, in a literature review, it is not simply good enough to offer a description of extant research and scholarly work relating to a predetermined topic, a literature review must engage in a discussion. Importantly, in this discussion, you want to stress how your research (proposed, forthcoming, or completed) builds on or fills in the gap in extant literature. To achieve this very goal, you must engage in juxtaposition.

A simple way to think about juxtaposition is envisioning your scholarly sources having a conversation with one another (i.e., synthesis) and through this conversation there is an ascend of a productive argument involving possible diverse evidence, results, and outcomes.

> **Exercise** With a peer or in a small group, read the following literature review and commentaries: https://westoahu.hawaii.edu/noeaucenter/wp-content/uploads/2019/10/Sample-Literature-Review.pdf. First discuss all the elements that must go into a literature review based on the example, starting with progression and structure, ensuring synthesis, and engaging in juxtaposition. Notice the topic, introduction, and conclusion. Then determine what might be the question that the author is answering by means of this literature review. After that, note the gaps that the author identified in the literature and determine what might be the author's forthcoming research study.

## 3.5 | Application: Annotated Bibliography—A Starting Point

Now that we reviewed how to make sense of the field, how to search for literature, and what constitutes a literature review, it is time to pause and apply your thus far knowledge in creating a tool that would assist with the literature review and serve as evidence-based professional reference—annotated bibliography. In this section, we will first define and then discuss how to construct an annotated bibliography.

An annotated bibliography is a collection of references comprised of a complete citation in APA and a brief summary of each source with annotations. The annotations are descriptive by nature and include an evaluation of each source. Annotated bibliographies are commonly used in one of two ways: (1) as a reference to assist with the literature review and (2) serve as an evidence-based reference. In both applications, annotated bibliographies are intended to serve as a valuable research *tool*—a hub of information for accessible and quick reference and to save time when constructing literature reviews.

To get you started on the path of writing an annotated bibliography, we outline the structure below. Each annotation should be brief and comprised of anywhere between five to ten sentences—as you construct each entry.

a. Start by including a **full citation in APA** at the top of each source
b. Proceed by writing a **summary** for each source. The summary portion should be two to four sentences in length and describe the main focus and/or purpose of the work. Consider the following questions: What is the topic covered? What is the research question(s)/hypothesis that the study aims to answer? What is the main argument? What are the results, conclusions, and limitations?
c. Evaluate each source. Your **evaluation** should be no more than three sentences. Start by objectively and critically evaluating each source and comment on how it compares with other sources in your bibliography. Include special features of the work that relate to your topic. State whether the source is current (i.e., within the last five to ten years) and whether you find it reliable (i.e., type of publication—see Table 3.1). Finally, and whenever possible, evaluate the credibility of the author, journal, and/or source of publication for credibility.
d. Conclude with a brief (one to two sentence) **reflection**. Your reflection should include take-aways, how this source has helped deepen or shape your thinking, how the source fits within your topic/research question(s), and how you might use this source in your literature review or practice.

Table 3.3: Annotate Bibliography Examples

| Source Type | APA 7th Annotated Bibliography Examples |
|---|---|
| Journal article | Alvarez, N., & Mearns, J. (2014). The benefits of writing and performing in the spoken word poetry community. *The Arts in Psychotherapy, 41*(3), 263–268. https://doi.org/10.1016/j.aip.2014.03.004<br><br>Prior research has shown narrative writing to help with making meaning out of trauma. This article uses grounded theory to analyze semi-structured interviews with ten spoken word poets. Because spoken word poetry is performed live, it creates personal and community connections that enhance the emotional development and resolution offered by the practice of writing. The findings are limited by the small, nonrandom sample (all the participants were from the same community). |
| Book | Ontiveros, R. J. (2014). *In the spirit of a new people: The cultural politics of the Chicano movement*. New York University Press.<br><br>Ontiveros argues that the arts provide an expression of the Chicano movement that circumvents neoliberalism and connects historic struggles to current lived experience. Chicano artists have integrated environmentalism and feminism with the Chicano movement in print media, visual arts, theater, and novels since the 1970s. Although focused on art, this book also provides a history of the coalition politics connecting the Chicano movement to other social justice struggles. |

*Source*: https://libguides.csun.edu/elementary-education/annotated-bib

## Abstracts Versus Annotations

By now, you have had an opportunity to read and review several academic articles, all of which begin with an abstract. The abstract is the author's summary of the article to help the reader decide whether reading the whole paper would be warranted. An abstract should not be confused with annotations. Annotations of scholarly articles only include a succinct summary and are primarily designed to provide an evaluation and reflection of a scholarly source to inform your topic of interest and help answer your research question(s).

## 3.6 | Conclusion

As we conclude Chapter 3, it is time to recap. Up to this point, you had an opportunity to review several empirical studies (Chapter 1), engage in your own search for literature (Section 3.3), examine the basics of a literature review (Section 3.4), and learn about an annotated bibliography (Section 3.5)—the *tool* needed to document review of scholarly sources. Naturally, the process itself is designed to guide you to circle back and reexamine your topic and research question(s) from the Plan of Action Part I assignment. This is a typical process that researchers engage in that help both sharpen the focus of a study and assist with narrowing down research question(s). It is not uncommon that this process of reexamination and search for information on a topic would lead one to revise their initial topic slightly, entirely, or not at all. If you are thinking about modifying your topic/research questions based on your new knowledge, you are not alone! In fact, it means you are learning.

In Section 3.2, we discussed the importance of peer review and peer professional opinion/support. Here we want to stress again that peer-review and peer-support are, in fact, foundational to sound research projects. Establishing a peer-review partnership or small group around a common interest will prove helpful moving forward, and we strongly suggest that you take advantage of an academic setting to benefit from such collaborations. As we conclude this chapter, we pose several questions for discussion and ask you to engage in a Plan of Action Part II assignment (a continuation of the Plan of Action).

## 3.7 | Discussion

1. Based on what is discussed, connect with your peers over your possible research question(s) or your theory of action. Then circle back and reflect on the indicator your questions are associated with.
2. Think about and describe a school best practice or practices that are directly related to your research question.
3. As you think though your research further, who do you think will be will be the audience of your potential research study?
4. Other than published articles, what OTHER sources (e.g., newspaper articles or even blogs) relate to your research question?

## 3.8 | Assignments: Plan of Action Part II and Human Subjects Certification

### Assignment 1: Plan of Action Part II

#### Instructions

Plan of Action Part II template is a continuation of the Part I assignment completed as part of Chapter 2. This assignment is the second building block of the starting process in conducting research. As a reminder, it is expected that you might rethink or revise your initial topic and/or research question(s) as you continue to engage with and conceptualize your project.

The following components to be included in this assignment *(delete all directions prior to submission)*:

CARRYOVER FROM PART I

- **State Indicator** *(revise as appropriate from Part I)*
- **Population of Focus** *(revise as appropriate from Part I)*
- **Topic** *(revise as appropriate from Part I)*
- **Overarching Question** *(revise as appropriate from Part I)*
  - **Specific Research Questions** *(as applicable)*

NEW

- **Search for Scholarly Sources**
- **Annotated Bibliography Based on Search**

*As a general reminder, it is perfectly fine and expected that you change, expand upon and/or revise/ modify your sources, topic, or questions as you learn more. And, the purpose of this assignment is to go through an exercise—that is, you are not firmly committing to this list and/or topics, but rather working through the process of engaging in research and using research as a tool.*

> ### Carryover from Plan of Action Part I
>
> *(Revise as needed/appropriate based on newly acquired knowledge OR if no revisions are warranted, complete these sections accordingly)*
>
> **State Indicator**
>
> _____
>
> **Population of Focus**
>
> _____
>
> **Topic**
>
> _____
>
> **Overarching Question**
>
> _____
>
> **Research Questions**
>
> 1. _____
> 2. _____
> 3. _____
>
> ### New Engagements
>
> **Scholarly Works**
>
> This exercise is designed to start the process of having you think about and investigate relevant literature that aligns with your selected topic and research questions. Although there is no limit on how many references/sources you list in this section, anywhere between five and ten are expected at this juncture. As part of an exercise in Section 3.3, we asked that you search for scholarly literature and save these articles in a designated place to be used later. If you have engaged in this exercise earlier, you are ready to construct your annotated bibliography. However, if you are yet to start/finalize your academic literature search or would like to revisit your initial search, please do this before the next step in the process.
>
> **Annotated Bibliography**
>
> Once you find at least scholarly sources (please remember that most of your search should consist of peer-reviewed, empirical articles/sources), use the step-by-step process for writing an annotated bibliography outlined in Section 3.5 to construct your annotated bibliography. You are also welcome to rely on the examples provided in this chapter.

## References

Alvarez, N., & Mearns, J. (2014). The benefits of writing and performing in the spoken word poetry community. *The Arts in Psychotherapy, 41*(3), 263–268. https://doi.org/10.1016/j.aip.2014.03.004

Ontiveros, R. J. (2014). *In the spirit of a new people: The cultural politics of the Chicano movement.* New York University Press.

# CHAPTER 4

# Quantitative Research and Application

*When and how do I use quantitative research to understand school practices?*

## 4.1 | Introduction

In this chapter, we discuss quantitative research and, more specifically, frequently occurring constructs in quantitative research. As a reminder, quantitative refers to a quantity or data requiring counting in any analyses. Educational researchers and practitioners frequently refer to quantitative data and studies as a way to look at disparities in education, better understand student performance and outcomes, as well as identify best classroom techniques and strategies. Your ability to recognize these basic concepts will provide a clearer understanding of how mathematical procedures can estimate data points, understand school practices, and identify the significance in any particular intervention all of which will help you further engage with research as a tool for better practice.

## 4.2 | Defining Quantitative Research

Quantitative research can refer to any part of a process that involves data collection and analysis of numerical data—a quantitative researcher strives to find patterns and relationships using either descriptive or inferential statistics. Generally speaking, quantitative research is a **deductive** view of a relationship between theory and research. The approach typically begins with a hypothesis (see Chapter 2) and aims to examine patterns, associations and determine causality. Conversely, an inductive approach discussed later in the textbook (see Chapter 5) is generally associated with qualitative research and aims to generate a new theory based on researchers' findings. The use of deductive (in quantitative studies) and inductive (in qualitative studies) approaches discussed here is more of a rule of thumb than a set one—that is, it is not uncommon to come across quantitative studies that use inductive approach and vice versa, a qualitative study that relies on a deductive one. This said and circling back to quantitative research, there is a general protocol or steps in quantitative research, which involve the following:

> Deductive refers to the process of starting with a theory and then testing the theory through analysis – usually quantitative.

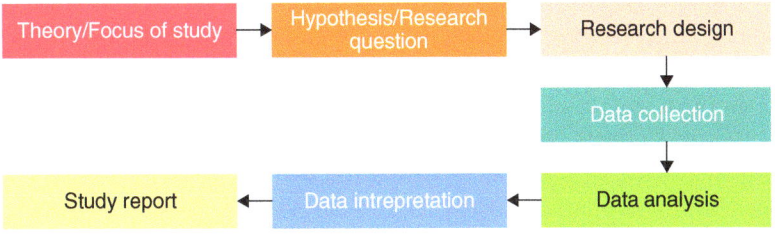

In the world of schools, there is more than enough quantitative data to go around. Educators are often confronted with student performance and demographic data, attendance data, behavioral data, among other data. There is so much quantitative data that it can be overwhelming, especially when one is puzzled about what to do with these data! There is little to no doubt that whether you are in a position of a classroom teacher, general educator, school leader, or administrator, you will be frequently asked to work with quantitative data on a regular, if not daily, basis. Likewise, you will be asked to examine, interpret, analyze data, and then determine the next steps to improve instructional practices in your classroom or set improvement goals for the entire school, its student body, and subgroups. In other words, you will be asked to use data to inform decisions. Thus, having the knowledge and tools necessary to find, organize and examine quantitative data even in the most basic descriptive ways (also see Chapter 2) will make your job much easier and more enjoyable.

## 4.3 | Quantitative Research

### *How to Describe What You See in So Many Numbers?*

At this point, you have read about the importance of looking at data and the understanding meaning from the information being presented. As human learners, most brains prefer to create categories and find patterns to make meaning (Seger, 2010).

For example, you have administered a fictional assessment test to decide what type of math exercises to assign to the 31 students in your classroom. The validated test instructions indicate that typical scores for 6th grade range between 62 and 100, with an average score of 80. The instructions also indicate that students that score 82 and less perform better with Unit A and those scoring above 82 perform better with Unit B. After scoring your 6th grade class, you see the results are:

97, 93, 94, 71, 85, 86, 82, 89, 83, 94, 79, 70, 91, 69, 68, 93,
82, 77, 69, 82, 80, 93, 82, 81, 76, 86, 85, 80, 84, 77, 74.

And while the scoring application tells you the average score for your class was 82, it doesn't give you much other information. Knowing that it is difficult to understand these numbers in random order without sorting them, you take the next step:

68, 69, 69, 70, 71, 74, 76, 77, 77, 79, 80, 80, 81, 82, 82, 82,
82, 83, 84, 85, 85, 86, 86, 89, 91, 93, 93, 93, 94, 94, 97.

Now, that you have sorted the scores, you are beginning to see that the scores for your 6th grade class fall into the validated range; the range for your class is 68 to 97. Further you see that 17 students will get Unit A and the remaining 14 students will get Unit B.

This simple example demonstrates how humans engage various cognitive processes to make meaning out of seemingly random data. By disaggregating the data and creating meaning out of these data—categorizing, sorting, scoring—you now have actionable information.

### Remembering Percentiles

Many tests in education, whether assessment tests or performance tests, display percentiles as a way of characterizing results. Percentiles state the percentage of the values which fall BELOW a particular value in the data—They are simply a way of placing a value in a wider context. For example, with the data above, we can recognize that 10% of students had scores in the 60s, 23% had scores in the 70s, 45% had scores in the 80s, and 23% had scores in the 90s. A student with a score in the 90s would have scored as well as or better than XX% of the class. We calculate this by adding the percentages in the lower scoring groups:

10% + 23% + 45% + half of 23% (11.5%) = 89.5%. In other words, this student scored higher than 89.5% of the class on this assessment. With this dataset, it might be easier to create quartiles, where you divide the scores into equal groups of four. Or deciles . . . groups of ten, and so on.

## Independent and Dependent Variables

Earlier, in Chapter 2, variables were discussed, let's circle back to that discussion. A variable is simply something that can be measured. As is evident by its label, a variable's value may change. For example, the amount of time someone studies, the hours of REM (Rapid Eye Movement) sleep you might get, the number of vitamins in your food, and so on. Sometimes, a variable doesn't have to be a number, it can be a name (i.e., a category).

> **Food for thought** What factors do you think might lead to higher scores on the fictional assessment test above? Brainstorm up to five and share/discuss with a peer or small group.

As educators, and school leaders, you can visualize a multitude of factors that lead to performance scores on standardized assessments. Some of these factors can be physical ones: Did the student get enough sleep, is the student sick, does the student have a hearing loss? Other factors could be behavioral: What is the cognitive level of the student, do they have special learning needs, does the student have test anxiety, is the student depressed? Also, the home environment of a student can influence test scores: Is the student's home language other than English, do caretakers read to the student or with the student, do caretakers support study time at home? Among other possible factors that impact student performance on standardized assessments.

Considering the above, if researchers were to set up a study to see if the factors above influence scoring outcomes, they would consider those as independent variables. That is, because the outcome (the test score) is dependent on these variables, the test score itself is the dependent variable. One way to visualize this relationship is through a conceptual model distinguishing dependent variable from that of independent variable, conceptually presented in Figure 4.1 below.

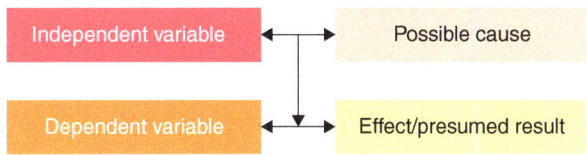

Figure 4.1: Independent Versus Dependent Variable

Another easy way to remember which variables are independent and which are dependent is to ask yourself, "which variable changes in response to another variable"? If the outcome varies in response to other variables, the outcome is a dependent variable. Independent variables are the ones that get manipulated (i.e., amount of sleep).

> **Food for thought** In a small group or with a partner, circle back to your Plan of Action assignments, and brainstorm dependent and independent variables as these relate to your topics/research questions independently first and then share with a partner/group to flash-out for accuracy and prior to discussing with instructor.

## Randomizing Sample

As a reminder, sampling is an important step when conducting research. It is the act of taking a subsection of the population of interest for your study instead of administering data collection for the entire population. The method of selecting this sample is so critical to a study that it is always mentioned in journal articles, oftentimes, even in the study abstract.

One key supposition of researchers when designing a sample is that it be representative of the population. For example, perhaps you would like to conduct a survey of all public school principals in the United States. The National Center for Education Statistics (NCES) reported 90,850 public school principals in the 2017 to 2018 school year (National Center for Education Statistics, 2019).

Administering a survey to this "universe" of principals would be a staggering amount of work, quite costly and, more importantly, with good sampling, not needed. Therefore, a typical approach is to select a subgroup to represent the population. The key to this sample being representative is that every member of the subgroup must have the same probability of being selected. The assumption in this probability sampling method is that the random selection of sample accurately represents the universe of principals. Referring to our NCES data table, we can expect that about 40% of public school principals are aged 50 or older. Your random sample should accurately reflect that distribution also as well as other characteristics such as gender and age to proportionally stratify the sample for accurate representation (more on sampling in Chapter 10).

It is important to note that not all surveys use a random sample design—there are many reasons why you might want to create a "nonprobability" design. This is a particularly useful sample method when looking for hard-to-find populations. For example, a study of LGBTQ principals: a complete list of this population does not exist somewhere from which to randomly sample. You may institute a "snowball sample" method to find respondents that meet your definition. This is where you ask your respondents to generate your sample by asking if they know of any other LGBTQ principals that could answer your survey. With this nonrandom method you cannot calculate the probability of being selected, but it is more feasible to find your population of interest.

There are many other types of nonprobability sampling designs descriptions for which you can easily find online by entering keywords: "nonprobability sampling." This said, we want to draw your attention to the most commonly used design in the field of Education often utilized by practitioner–researchers, which is "convenience sampling." As the name explains, this is a sample method that is most convenient for the researcher and, therefore, easiest to implement.

That is, you survey your friends, peers at your school, or even strangers at the mall. It is important to keep in mind that this type of sampling does not necessarily create results that are representative of the larger population, but it is a perfectly acceptable method to better understand the population that is accessible. To minimize any bias, a researcher can replicate the study in other settings and use probability sample to cross-validate findings.

## Validity and Reliability

The concepts of validity and reliability are often confused—but they have very independent meaning. These measures are key indicators of the quality of a particular instrument (i.e., survey). When experienced researchers wish to answer a research question, they will look for tests or instruments that have been validated and found to be reliable. Validity refers to the concept that something is measuring what it is intended to measure. For example, in Figure 4.2, researchers Amy Doolittle and Ann Faul wanted to test different types of validity for the measure of the Civic Engagement Scale (Doolittle & Faul, 2013).

**Exercise** In a small group, first read the abstract aloud. Then read it again. As you read through the abstract for the second time, take note of a few keywords. After that, using your favorite search engine, look up the terms you are not familiar with. Examples might include: purposive; subscale; Cronbach's alpha; factor loading. As you better understand the information presented in the abstract, make an educated opinion regarding the authors' stated limitations of the study? Do you agree with the conclusion that this scale would be a useful one?

**Civic Engagement Scale: A Validation Study**

Amy Doolittle, Anna C. Faul

First Published July 4, 2013 | Research Article | https://doi.org/10.1177/2158244013495542

Article information ⌄

**Abstract**

This study reports on the development and validation of the Civic Engagement Scale (CES). This scale is developed to be easily administered and useful to educators who are seeking to measure the attitudes and behaviors that have been affected by a service-learning experience. This instrument was administered as a validation study in a purposive sample of social work and education majors at three universities ($N = 513$) with a return of 354 (69%). After the reliability and validity analysis was completed, the Attitude subscale was left with eight items and a Cronbach's alpha level of .91. The Behavior subscale was left with six items and a Cronbach's alpha level of .85. Principal component analysis indicated a two-dimensional scale with high loadings on both factors (mean factor loading for the attitude factor $= .79$, and mean factor loading for the behavior factor $= .77$). These results indicate that the CES is strong enough to recommend its use in educational settings. Preliminary use has demonstrated that this scale will be useful to researchers seeking to better understand the relationship of attitudes and behaviors with civic engagement in the service-learning setting. The primary limitations of this research are that the sample was limited to social work and education majors who were primarily White ($n = 312$, 88.1%) and female ($n = 294$, 83.1%). Therefore, further research would be needed to generalize this research to other populations.

Figure 4.2: Testing Different Types of Validity for the Measures in the Civic Engagement Scale
Source: (Doolittle & Faul, 2013)

Now, if validity is the statistical assertion that a measure is truly measuring what it claims to measure, what is reliability? Here is a concrete example that many could relate to: If a principal says her teachers are reliable, we immediately understand that they show up to class regularly, are prepared for the day, and will consistently perform their duties—simply put, reliable.

Likewise, we can think of a reliable instrument or measure in a similar way: It is going to produce the same results over time and with repeated measures. Would you consider a scale at the doctor's office reliable if upon repeated, successive measures there was a ten-pound variability? No. Similar to testing for validity, researchers can test for reliability. See this excerpt from the same Civic Engagement Scale study (Figure 4.3).

> **Reliability**
>
> To begin the validation phase, the instrument was examined for reliability. The coefficient alpha was used to determine the reliability estimate. To create a scale that can be easily used, it was important to create an instrument with as few items as possible with the highest alpha coefficient possible. The attitude component was left with eight items from the original 11 items with a Cronbach's alpha level of .91. The behavior component was left with six items from the original 11 items with a Cronbach's alpha level of .85. The final items are presented in the appendix. These findings supported the internal consistency of the subscales. The strongest attitude items were "I am committed to serve in my community" and "I believe that all citizens have a responsibility to their community." The strongest behavior items were "I help members of my community" and "I stay informed of events in my community."

**Figure 4.3:** Testing for Reliability in the Civic Engagement Scale

Here, the researchers found that they only needed a subset of the original items on the measure to get reliable results. Because only a subset of items is needed, the researchers have discovered a more parsimonious measure. In other words, they have unearthed a simpler method with fewer variables needed to draw conclusions about the sample. Not only does this reduce the "respondent burden" but identifies the variables that carry the most explanatory influence.

> **Food for thought** Why do you think researchers want the most parsimonious measure possible? In other words, why would a researcher be interested in shortening the length of an instrument? Finally, an instrument that has validity is not necessarily reliable, and vice versa. Can you think of examples of this?

## Significance: The Cousin to Probability

Significance is perhaps the most widely misunderstood concept in research. Simply stated, statistical significance is a statistical measure of whether a detected difference is due to chance (probability) or whether it is due to an actual relationship between two (or more) variables. Essentially, that is the work of all research: is there a real relationship between specific factors? Of course, there are a multitude of statistical tests—some quite complex—to ascertain whether a relationship is "significant," that is, not caused by random chance.

The most common/universal measure of significance is listed as a "$p$" value—because it is a measure of probability. Researchers want to find a very small $p$ value in their results: the smaller the $p$ value, the less likely the relationship is due to chance. And while many scientists caution about relying on $p$ values to state something is "true," the correct interpretation is that there is a certain amount of chance (even a small one) that this outcome occurred in error.

Okay—"what?" you may be asking . . . Look at the example below (Figure 4.4): scientists/researchers usually consider a $p$ value of .05 or smaller as an indication that the relationship is not likely due to random chance. The actual interpretation should be that this result will occur by chance 5% of the time (Pogrow, 2019).

# Chapter 4: Quantitative Research and Application

> The recession significantly affected suburban school districts, which experienced a statistically significant drop (β = −0.19, t = 2.75, p < .01) in percentage of budget allocated toward gifted funding following the recession. The rate of funding change following the recession did not vary among locales.

**Figure 4.4:** Excerpt Showing Use of *p* Value as Sign of Significance

Source: (Hodges et al., 2018)

Math to Watch out for:

- Large sample sizes are not always helpful in research; with a large enough sample you can detect the smallest level of difference and call if significant.
- Small sample sizes—often seen in education research—may not reveal a relationship when there really is one.
- Even a lack of statistical significance might have "clinical" significance. Imagine a new treatment for a degenerative disease does not meet the $p < .05$ level. Instead, the probability of the treatment showing a probable difference is $p < .10$.

## Correlation

This text has been discussing quantitative research outcomes as descriptions of relationships. This is particularly the case when looking at correlations. The strength of a correlation ranges from −1 to +1 (usually represented by the letter *r*). The closer *r* is to −1, the stronger is the negative correlation. A negative correlation describes the direction of the relationship between variables: As one integer increases, the other decreases. Logically, the closer *r* is to +1, the stronger is the positive correlation. This indicates that as one integer increases, the other one does also. An *r* value of 0 means there is no relationship. An *r* value of −1 or +1 indicates a perfect linear correlation. (see Figure 4.5).

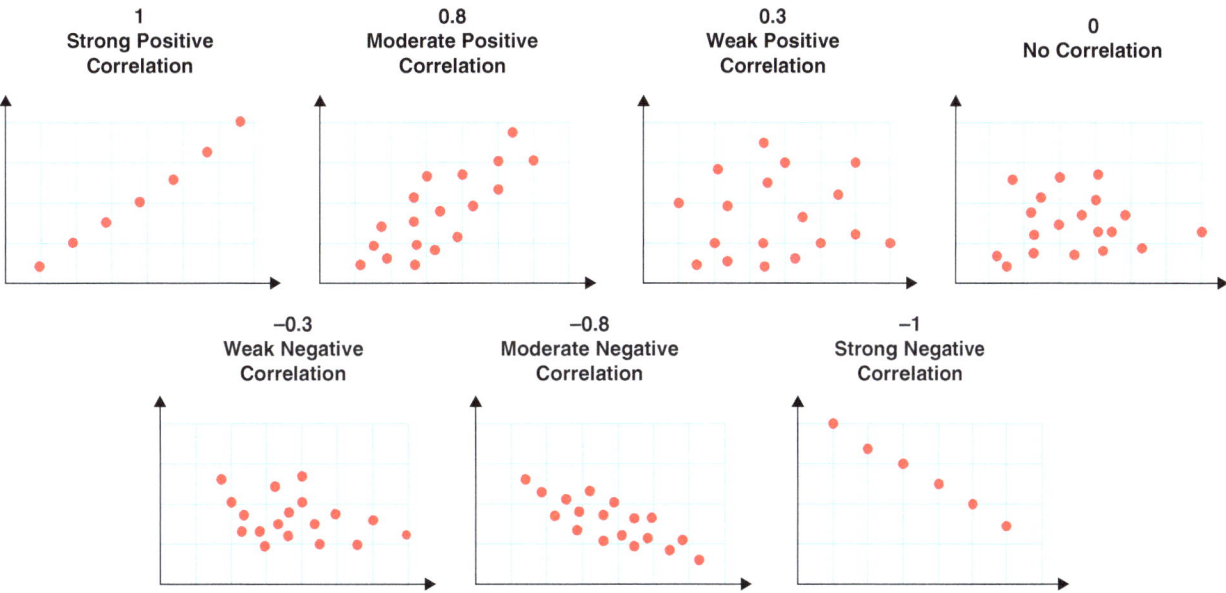

Correlation coefficient measures how strong the data fits a linear pattern. Correlation coefficient ranges from −1 to 1.

**Figure 4.5:** Pectoral Representation of Correlations Insert Chart of Examples Below

## 4.4 | Application

### When and How Do I Use Quantitative Research to Understand School Practices?

By revisiting your Plan of Action Part I and II assignments from Chapters 2 and 3, in this section, we ask that you apply your newly gained knowledge and expand on the examination of data from Chapter 2 application section by examining three years' worth of data. This examination of longitudinal data will help boost your understandings from an earlier search and aid in illustrating patterns in data for your chosen student subgroup as compared to other groups. Therefore, helping you acquire better knowledge about student performance overtime and a potential existing equity gap at the school site. At this juncture, you are welcome to engage in this search holistically by reviewing multiple patterns of data over the course of three years to further inform your topic and complete the Section 4.7 assignment later OR partake in a more focused exercise with the help of a template provided below in the assignment section.

**Table 4.1:** California Department of Education Data Sources

| Source (CDE) | Link to website |
| --- | --- |
| EdData | https://www.ed-data.org/ |
| DataQuest | https://dq.cde.ca.gov/dataquest/ |
| California School Dashboard | https://www.caschooldashboard.org/ |
| Local Control and Accountability Plan (LCAP) | https://www.cde.ca.gov/re/lc/ |
| School Accountability Report Card (SARC) | https://www.cde.ca.gov/ta/ac/sa/ |

To model this application exercise and assist in maneuvering through a database, we provide a step-by-step explanation using CDE's EdData. To be consistent with other examples in prior chapters, we are using our selected topic: ELL academic performance on mathematics as compared to their non-ELL/English-only counterparts. For that, we need to examine data for ELLs as well as other student subgroups over the course of several years (three years in this case) to truly understand possible equity concerns at the school site and beyond for our population of focus (ELLs).

**Step 1:** After gaining access to EdData website (https://www.ed-data.org/), we selected the county (Alameda), district (Alameda Unified), and the school of interest (Alameda High). By selecting "GO" the site directed us to the place depicting school's "Information" and "Key Attributes." Similarly, in your search, enter the county, district, and the school of interest for your chosen school. Once you click "GO" the page will depict alike school information and data for your chosen school.

**Step 2:** Once you find your school site, scroll down and select from the fields as appropriate based on your selected state indicator. Since for the purposes of this example, our focus is **academic performance**, we selected "Performance."

**Step 3:** As the focus of our topic is ELL performance on **mathematics**, we selected performance on "CAASPP Mathematics Results" and then from the scroll down "View by student group" menu we selected "CAASPP Mathematics Results for English Learners." Do note that your chosen topic and indicator might differ from ours, so expand and examine data relevant to your chosen topic.

**Step 4:** We are then able to see performance overtime in percentages with respect to EL performance on mathematics. Again, use these described steps as an example to find the quantitative data that aligns with your selected indicator and chosen topic/population of focus.

Now, it is important to remember that **to determine inequities in performance and, therefore, determine academic performance equity gap, it is not simply enough to examine performance of one student subgroup** (although a good place to start to narrow down your focus)—the question will always be, *performance as compared to whom?* Therefore, examining similar performance data for other subgroups, for example, by ethnicity, student needs, and so on, for the entire school, will provide needed points of comparison for future analysis. In the assignment section below, we include a template to help document quantitative patterns of data with respect to student performance and/or wellbeing. We ask that you use the information we provide in this application section to complete the assignment (Section 4.7). Additional directions are embedded in the assignment's template.

## 4.5 | Conclusion

This chapter provided an overview of key concepts in quantitative research and application that you would likely encounter and use across education research. By understanding the concepts presented in this chapter, you will be able to critically and productively examine research of others and formulate understandings about your own research of quantitative data, allowing you to make important determinations around which findings are meaningful for your particular application. Remembering again that research is a *tool* to reach for when you need to answer important questions in education. Many analytical concepts may be discussed in journals: from very basic to highly complex. However, the elements presented here will help you understand most published education research and engage in your own search and examination of quantitative data.

## 4.6 | Discussion

1. As you think about definition of quantitative research in Section 4.2, what are the three to five take-aways that resonated with you as a practitioner in the field? Why?
2. Reflecting on the discussion in Section 4.3: Where do you see correlations being helpful in looking at your data school and/or district? Where do you see these being a potential danger to use?
3. Reliability and validity of data are commonly used and confused terms. Give a practical example of where reliability could be confused with validity?
4. Create a list of the data that you understand to be collected daily in schools and the data that is collected annually. Of these data sets, what are different ways to use these data to inform practical school site-based decisions?
5. Think about and then provide up to three examples of how you would use quantitative data to drive decisions, make school site plans or improve instruction.

## 4.7 | Assignment: Quantitative Data Exercise & Synthesis

| Instructions Part 1 |
|---|
| The Quantitative Synthesis segment is your opportunity to take a closer look at the quantitative data and begin to examine equity concerns for your selected school site as these relate to your selected indicator, chosen topic, and population of focus.<br><br>*As a general reminder, through prior assignments (Plan of Action I & II) you will have selected a state indicator, determined a topic of interest, drafted a research question(s), and created an annotated bibliography as you searched for scholarly sources to further inform your knowledge of the selected topic.*<br><br>From the application section of this chapter, select the data source from Table 4.1 and follow the steps outlined in Section 4.4 to gather longitudinal quantitative data for the student populations and for the three different levels, that is, school site, district, and the state. Record quantitative data in the tables provided below for each of the student groups (*if all groups are not recorded in the school population, you may remove the column*) and three levels of data as available/reported (i.e., **school site**—*your main table and must be included*, district level—*as available*, and/or state level). As you find and input data, highlight your population of focus so it stands out in the recorded data the way you see fit (in our case we bolded "ELL").<br><br>*Remember each data source should include data for three years on your chosen indicator/topic of interest.* |

Data source/level (your main table/source of data): **School Site** (include topic, e.g., Academic Performance on Mathematics) *(cite your source per APA)*

| Indicator | All | **ELL** | Foster Youth | Homeless | SES | Special Ed | Am-Indian | Asian | Filipino | Latino | Pacific Islander | Two or more races | Black | White |
|---|---|---|---|---|---|---|---|---|---|---|---|---|---|---|
| Year 1 | | | | | | | | | | | | | | |
| Year 2 | | | | | | | | | | | | | | |
| Year 3 | | | | | | | | | | | | | | |

Data source/level: **School District** (include topic, e.g., Academic Performance on Mathematics) *(cite your source per APA)*

| Indicator | All | **ELL** | Foster Youth | Homeless | SES | Special Ed | Am-Indian | Asian | Filipino | Latino | Pacific Islander | Two or more races | Black | White |
|---|---|---|---|---|---|---|---|---|---|---|---|---|---|---|
| Year 1 | | | | | | | | | | | | | | |
| Year 2 | | | | | | | | | | | | | | |
| Year 3 | | | | | | | | | | | | | | |

Data source/level: **The State** (include topic, e.g., Academic Performance on Mathematics) *(cite your source per APA)*

| Indicator | All | ELL | Foster Youth | Homeless | SES | Special Ed | Am-Indian | Asian | Filipino | Latino | Pacific Islander | Two or more races | Black | White |
|---|---|---|---|---|---|---|---|---|---|---|---|---|---|---|
| Year 1 | | | | | | | | | | | | | | |
| Year 2 | | | | | | | | | | | | | | |
| Year 3 | | | | | | | | | | | | | | |

### Instructions Part 2

Once you have charted the data for student populations, develop a short synthesis of the data you have collected (*no more than a five-sentence paragraph for each of the data tables*). As you write your synthesis remember to identify equity-related trends between subgroups and/or patterns as observed and associated with your indicator/topic and population of focus. Provide a longitudinal (overtime/over the course of three years) evaluation of data for each of the levels. Use transition sentences to tie your paragraphs into a coherent and logical interpretations of the data you have collected—put differently, as you compose synthesis of data think of school staff as your audience: *What do patterns within or between different levels communicate about the topic/indicator and specifically the student subgroup as compared to all other groups? What trends and relationships do your colleagues and you must be aware of? and so on.*

## References

Doolittle, A., & Faul, A. C. (2013, July 1). Civic engagement scale: A validation study. *SAGE Open, 3*(3), 1–7. https://doi.org/10.1177/2158244013495542

Hodges, J., Tay, J., Desmet, O., Oturk, E., & Pereira, N. (2018, July 5). The effect of the 2008 recession on gifted education funding across the state of Texas. *AERA Open.* https://doi.org/10.1177%2F2332858418786224

National Center for Education Statistics. (2019). *Table 212.08. Number and percentage distribution of principals in public and private elementary and secondary schools, by selected characteristics: Selected years, 1993–94 through 2017–18.* Digest of Education Statistics. https://nces.ed.gov/programs/digest/d19/tables/dt19_212.08.asp

Pogrow, S. (2019). How effect size (practical significance) misleads clinical practice: The case for switching to practical benefit to assess applied research findings. *The American Statistician, 73,* 223–234. https://www.tandfonline.com/doi/full/10.1080/00031305.2018.1549101

Seger, C. M. (2010). Category learning the brain. *Annual Review of Neuroscience, 33,* 203–219. https://doi.org/10.1146/annurev.neuro.051508.135546

# CHAPTER 5

# Qualitative Research and Applications

*When and how do I use qualitative research to inform school practices?*

## 5.1 | Introduction

Qualitative research is a preferred methodology when researchers are interested in the deeper context of a population of interest by asking, *What are the systems in which this population exists?* This very question is often at the core of qualitative research and qualitative work. As we unpack qualitative research in this chapter, we discuss several types of qualitative research methods in education, cover researcher's responsibilities, and how researchers position themselves as a participant or observer during qualitative data collection—their positionality. As part of this discussion, that is, researcher's positionality, and ethical responsibility, we ask you to partake in online training to make you Institutional Review Board (IRB) eligible to conduct research (Section 5.6). Finally, we conclude this chapter with an assignment designed to put your newly learned qualitative skills to work.

## 5.2 | Defining Qualitative Research

There are misperceptions that qualitative research is somehow less rigorous, or less fact-based than quantitative research. Yet, **qualitative research**, when done well, can take far more time, analysis, and effort to execute than a quantitative study. With its roots in anthropological research, qualitative research often involves the investigator having a relationship with the source. Also, qualitative research typically involves far more writing and studious interaction with collected data. Qualitative methodologies often used in the field of education include: ethnography, case studies, and grounded theory, all of which rely on the inductive approach. We unpack all three in this chapter.

When we discuss qualitative research as a way of describing "contexts," researchers are really wanting to gather richer, more meaningful data. In Chapter 4, we briefly mentioned the inductive approach in qualitative research to offer a comparison to another approach, deductive (see Chapters 2 and 4), that is often used in quantitative research. We want to remind all that although there are no set rules of application for the two approaches (i.e., deductive and inductive), the inductive approach is mainly applied in qualitative research and is most referenced in Grounded Theory (see Section 5.3). The key aspect of applying this approach is that it requires researchers to embark on their qualitative investigation without any preconceived ideas of what they will find. Keeping a completely open mind during a qualitative investigation will ensure a more authentic explanation and a greater chance of generating a new theory as evidenced in the data (Corbin & Anselm, 1990).

Therefore, an inductive approach is often, if not always, the approach used in qualitative methodologies. Inductive is the approach employed when you use your data to develop a theory—compared to deductive, which is an experiment to test a theory

> Deductive approach: An experiment to test a theory
>
> Inductive approach: Use data collected to develop a theory

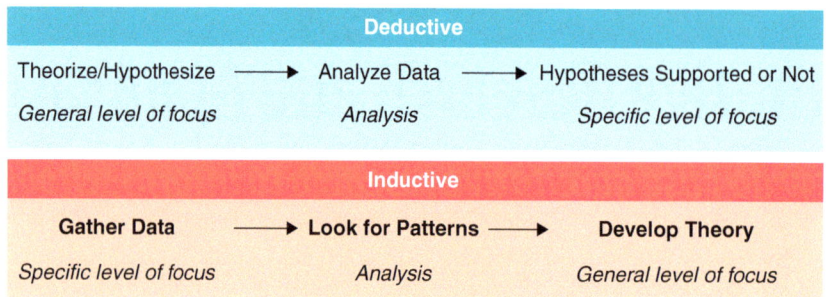

**Figure 5.1:** Deductive Pathway in Research Versus Inductive Pathway

Adapted from Blackstone. (2012). *Principals of sociological inquiry: Qualitative and quantitative methods.* Saylor Foundation.

## Researcher's Responsibilities When Conducting Qualitative Research

As we unpack the most popular types of qualitative research in education: case studies, interviews, ethnographies, and so on, it is imperative to consider that we must examine our responsibility as researchers. It is critical to not treat subjects as "other": the humans we interact with as we engage in research must not feel that they are objects of curiosity or "ownership" but, instead, that we aim to understand the contextual reality of an education setting better. As researchers, we must not deny the reality that we may hold privilege and power as we seek to understand the context of education research and practice.

Another essential component to remember is that most qualitative research (the exception being content analysis) involves the human element. This said, however, interacting with humans is not always a necessity of qualitative research. Hence, for those researchers who prefer to observe a context rather than interact with humans, an observer effect still exists that can influence the behaviors of research subjects and, therefore, must be considered.

## Decolonizing Research

As we consider the researcher's responsibilities when conducting qualitative research, we (as researchers) must also be acutely aware of the historical underpinnings of research. Therefore, as part of the application section (Section 5.6) of this chapter, we ask that you complete the Human Subjects training to understand the history of research and the potential harm that research can cause. The training is necessary to understand the researcher's responsibility from a more learned perspective and begin thinking about research in decolonizing ways.

Decolonizing research (and researcher) in education is the concept that research, methodology, and institutions themselves are colonizing products of oppressive systems of scholarship (Patel, 2016). The term is often discussed in relationship of indigenous people to researcher with colonial reproduction in education research; reinforcing racism and notions of white supremacy by unquestioning privilege and accepting existing structures in education. Indigenous scholars not only want to bring these institutionalized inequalities to light, but vociferously condemn coloniality in education and education research.

Indigenous scholars advance this decolonizing discourse by suggesting that "Western-centric knowledge production" could be "co-created jointly between Indigenous and Western researchers" allowing Indigenous perspectives to define their own standards of knowledge production (Thambinathan & Kinsella, 2021). Researchers must acknowledge their own positionality in the context of the research and the researched.

## 5.3 | Grounded Theory

Grounded Theory (Glaser & Strauss, 1967) is one of the most well-known and utilized research methodologies in research. Although grounded theory prides itself in its flexibility, the methodology itself is quite complex. Although primarily used in qualitative research, grounded theory is positioned to construct theory from data through comparative analysis; therefore, quantitative data generation techniques could also be applied in a grounded theory study.

Perhaps the best contemporary framework depicting a comprehensive summary of the interplay between the essential methods and processes related to grounded theory is attributed to Chun et al. (2019). This framework is represented in Figure 5.2. As you review the involved process of the framework, the authors stress that grounded theory is not a linear process but rather an interplay between comparative actions involved.

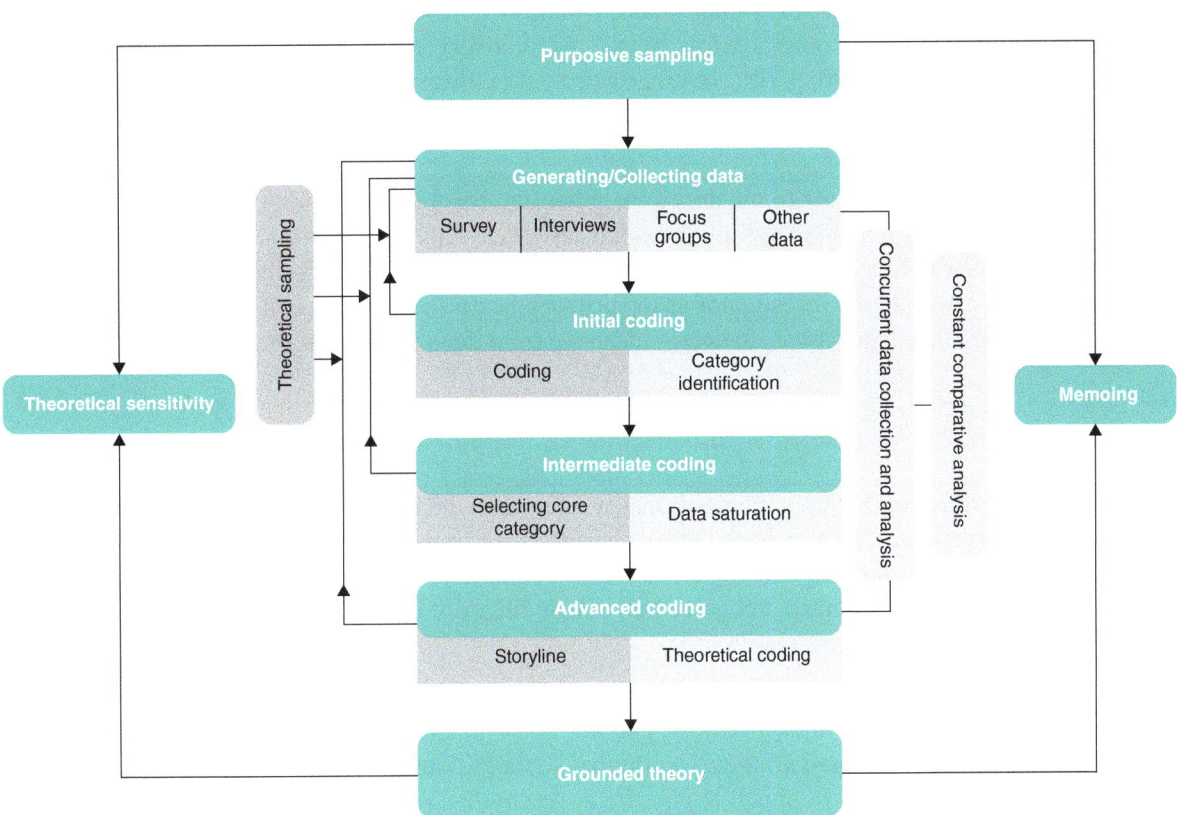

**Figure 5.2:** Research Design Framework: Summary of the Interplay Between the Essential Grounded Theory Methods and Processes Adapted from: https://www.ncbi.nlm.nih.gov/pmc/articles/PMC6318722/figure/fig1-2050312118822927/

Throughout the inquiry process, grounded theory requires the discipline of researchers to be consistently self-reflexive and to position themselves in the framing of the iterative development of a resulting theory. This process has been defined as a "self-correcting approach that integrates research processes—such as collecting data, defining subsequent samples, coding data, analysing [sic] data, writing memos and diagrams, generating theory, and reviewing literature—in cyclic and cumulative ways so that emerging concepts can be explored further" (Birks & Mills, 2012, p. 174).

For comparison purposes, let us circle back to the deductive nature of quantitative research (see Chapters 2 & 4) where researchers start with a hypothesis then develop a way to "test" the hypothesis using numerical measures. Qualitative research, on the other hand, is often used to "develop" a hypothesis from a researcher's own subjective experience with the subject(s)—based on inductive reasoning. We ask that you recall the hypothesis we posed in Chapter 2 where an administrator wished to test their hypothesis that establishing parental affinity groups outside of school hours will increase parental participation in school-related activities. Using quantitative research methods, this administrator launches parental affinity groups and, using numerical analyses, deduces the outcomes based on statistical evaluation.

Now, let us assume that another administrator, also hoping to increase parental participation in school-related activities, decides to take a qualitative approach. This administrator decides to interview parents (based upon an interview protocol) that rarely attend school events. The collected interview responses are then reviewed and analyzed to see how best to begin to build a hypothesis based upon the respondents' answers. As one researcher noted, "qualitative research often takes the position that an interpretive understanding is only possible by way of uncovering or deconstructing the meanings of a phenomenon" (Thorne, 2000, p. 68). In other words, it is through the subjective experience of researchers with the data they collect from their informants that they create meaning from their discoveries.

Yet another administrator is looking to the data to help her develop a theory as to existing barriers for parents to increase their participation at school-related activities. This type of research method relies on the data collected to create a theory; therefore, "grounded theory"—it is grounded in data. "As is true in other forms of qualitative research, the investigator as the primary instrument of data collection and analysis assumes an inductive stance and strives to derive meaning from the data" (Merriam, 1998, p. 17).

## 5.4 | Positionality

Positionality refers to the researcher's intersectionality relative to the multiple contexts of a study (Coghlan & Brydon-Miller, 2014). In other words, the researcher has a particular position in respect to the multiple contexts of a study; "the community, the organization or the participant group" (Coghlan & Brydon-Miller, 2014, p. 80). As researchers, we must recognize that our findings are informed by our own subjectivities in the course of conducting qualitative research.

Qualitative research is sometimes called interpretive research—eschewing the rigid notion that there is one truth, but rather multiple interpretations that are constructed in contexts (Merriam & Tisdell, 2016). It is not difficult to understand the evolution of socially constructed contexts in qualitative research to another type of philosophical lens: critical research. "Today, critical research draws from feminist theory, critical race theory, postcolonial theory, queer theory, critical ethnography, and so on. In critical inquiry the goal is to critique and challenge, to transform and empower" (Merriam & Tisdell, 2016, p. 10). Critical research requires us to examine our own relationships of power, negotiation, and privilege.

Postmodernism can be considered another type of research epistemology—where there is no single truth—no linear life trajectory. Critical discourse analysis emerged from postmodern theoretical frameworks where researchers, "critically questioning power dynamics, structures, and their consequent discourses, which is necessary for educators to embrace as we continue to examine the function of education" (Campbell, 2018).

## 5.5 | Approaches and Types of Qualitative Research in Education

> **Exercise** Self-reflexive questions
> 1. In what ways can qualitative researchers position themselves in their study?
> 2. How can researchers be more reflexive of bias—their own bias?
> 3. What do you think of the notion that one can co-create research with their subjects?
> 4. Which of the four theoretical approaches resonates with how you would approach education research? Positivist, Interpretive, Critical, Post-Modern.
> 5. What does it mean to have power as a researcher?

### Observations

Whether quantitative or qualitative, researchers often use the word "observation." This word can mean varying things in varying contexts, so the authors wish to make clear about this definition as used in qualitative studies. In quantitative research, an observation refers to a study participant. No matter if a survey is short or has 200 data points, those 200 data points belong to each observation. Software often presents an observation number as a row, with data points as the columns. This might also be called a "structured observation."

In any study, the research question drives the type of observation needed to collect the appropriate type of data. Oftentimes, the qualitative researcher may create tools for collecting semi-structured, or even unstructured observations. Semi-structured observation might include a list of open-ended questions to be asked of everyone; or there may be some definite questions with space allowed for unplanned responses (Jamshed, 2014). Focus groups can fall into this category; a group of respondents is convened, and a facilitator/moderator asks certain questions to spark a greater discussion.

There does exist the concept of "unstructured" observation, but this rarely occurs in contemporary field research. In unstructured observation, a researcher would let the participant guide the direction—one can imagine this in long-term fieldwork where there is only a vague research question.

### Observer Effect

In qualitative research, the researcher is the primary instrument of the data collected. Tropes of impartiality and objectivity are challenged when we recognize that our mere presence in a study can influence the data collected. Some researchers have expressed concern that as observers and data collectors, investigators run the risk of not only influencing study participants, but that participants might also affect the investigator, and that these interactions might occur unknowingly. Certainly, some social psychologists have expressed concern that observer effect (or observer bias, expectancy bias, experimenter bias) can lead to erroneous conclusions. For example, a teacher being observed in her classroom may act in ways that are more socially acceptable to present herself more favorably to the observer.

In an early exploration of the topic, Stephen Wilson (1977) asserted that qualitative researchers must make themselves a "sensitive research instrument by transcending his [sic] own perspective" (p. 261) and understanding the perspective of the participants. This perspective rejects the notion that observers must strive to remain objective and detached from the participants, but rather that, "some of the greatest strengths of ethnographic research lie in cultivating close ties with others . . . Informants' performances—however staged for or influenced by the observer—often reveal profound truths about social and/or cultural phenomena" (Monahan & Fisher, 2010).

## Interviews

The predominant form of collecting data for qualitative research studies is through interviews. In quantitative research, interviews are typically highly structured and strictly administered in a standardized manner. These types of standardized questions might also be asked in a qualitative study, however, usually these are in regard to respondent information (i.e., age, race, occupation, income, etc.). In a qualitative interview, the questions posed may run a wider breadth: from highly structured to highly unstructured. The types of questions developed will depend upon the depth of information a researcher wants to collect.

**Table 5.1:** Types of Interview Questions

| Type | Characteristics | Content | Used in | Type of Research | Pros | Cons |
|---|---|---|---|---|---|---|
| Highly structured, Standardized | Read every word; ask question in same order and same way for each respondent | Response options are usually predetermined and hard-coded (i.e., closed-ended) | Phone surveys; Web surveys; Marketing | Quantitative | Take less time, collect large amounts of data, already coded for analysis | Little context of respondent's situations |
| Semi-structured | May include mixed question types and allow for some flexibility | Mix of some predetermined response options | Focus groups, Key Informant Interviews | Quantitative, Qualitative, Mixed | Ability to gather range of topics with some specificity | Two types of analyses to plan and undertake |
| Unstructured | Very flexible | Open-ended questions; protocol developed to guide questions | Case studies; ethnographies | Qualitative, Mixed | Deep, rich understanding of respondent's context, free-flowing—may lead to unexpected directions; conversational | Analyses are more time consuming |

Researchers may spend years perfecting questions for various types of studies. It is beyond the scope of this chapter to discuss in-depth questionnaire or interview protocol development. However, there are some important guideposts.

> Do not ask more than one question at a time; for example "What do you think about the new principal and the new school policies?"
>
> Do not ask leading questions; for example, "How difficult has it been to implement the new curriculum?"
>
> Avoid Yes-or-No (dichotomous) questions, especially if you wish to elicit a thoughtful response. For example, "Did you learn something from the training?"

Qualitative interviewing requires trust between the researcher and participants. You can gain trust by getting consent to interview them. If you intend to record the interview, this must be discussed as part of the consent process. Also, the data gathered must be held to the highest levels of confidentiality approved through your Human Subject Research review board and discussed in your informed consent.

Whether undertaking a case study or ethnography, qualitative interviewing in Education is often a useful method to discover what cannot be understood or perceived by observation alone. One sociologist—expert in qualitative interviews—looking at the social construction of education says, "The interview is, in short, a model of dialectically emergent social relations" (Kalekin-Fishman, 2002, p. 2). Whether employing focus groups, key informant interviews, cognitive interviews, or narrative interviews for a study, interviews are one of three important data-collection methods in qualitative inquiry: observation and document reviews being the others.

## Case Studies

Examples of case studies in education are plentiful. One underused source for literature reviews is dissertation works, where case studies are a popular form of research. Case studies are appropriate forms of research when intensely studying one individual or one phenomenon. They can also be useful when studying a group or "unit" (Gustafsson, 2017). A case study is not a methodology, but describes a unit of interest, in its own complex setting. In fact, Yin describes a case study as, "an empirical inquiry that investigates a contemporary phenomenon in depth and within its real-life context, especially when the boundaries between phenomenon and context are not clearly evident" (Yin, 2009, p. 18).

Case studies typically involve multiple types of data collection from multiple sources. Certainly, interviewing is one type of data collection activity. However, as a case study has a limited population of interest it becomes necessary to triangulate (or validate) information from other sources. For example, one case study revealed during an interview that an administrator was very proud of their "diversity hires" and that most of the new teachers they onboarded were people of color. In looking at administrative records, however, the documentation revealed that they only onboarded two non-White teachers out of the six they hired that year. This contradiction reveals a complexity that would be hidden had the data not been triangulated. Furthermore, this constructed incongruity helps the researcher better understand the way "people make sense of their world" (Yazan, 2015).

## Ethnographies

Whereas case studies are useful in education research to build a detailed understanding of a single person, unit, or phenomenon, ethnographies are an effective form of qualitative research to study a culture or society (Merriam, 1998). This method originated in anthropological research and in education it is employed for similar purposes—to better understand the culture of a particular community or group in its sociocultural context. An ethnographic study of a new migrant population in a high school would also incorporate the shared community experience of migration, the neighborhood, shared language, and so on.

## Content Analysis

This type of data-collection technique has some quantitative elements but is a qualitative method at its core. The idea behind this technique is to look at primary sources and create categories that are then counted. In this way, a researcher can indirectly study a topic of interest. A researcher can look through all types of content: books, magazines, social media, movies, journals, meeting minutes, and so on. For example, one can create categories of how school principals are portrayed in popular films over the last 30 years and tally the observations. Another possibility is to watch videotape of teachers and count their interactions with quiet children and comparing interactions with more outspoken students. Collecting this type of data can help reveal shifting attitudes over time or challenge points in crowded classrooms. Chapter 7 of this text will discuss qualitative data analysis in more detail.

## 5.6 | Application: Human Subjects Certification

Please note that the certification process will take anywhere between three and four hours. Therefore, we suggest planning for this engagement ahead of time to allow for the time needed to complete the application section of this chapter.

1. Got to: https://about.citiprogram.org/ once on the page, select **"Register"** on the right-hand side

Select your organization from the list and proceed through the registration and training.

## 5.7 | Conclusion

In this chapter, we covered some of the building blocks in qualitative research. After reading through this chapter, one can see that qualitative research takes a significant amount of time, planning, and thought, even before the final analysis can take place. As we discuss these concepts, our goal is to introduce you to critical *tools* in conducting qualitative research. Section 5.9 provided a template and instructions in helping you design the instruments you will need for qualitative data collection. We want to reinforce the idea that while you are conducting research, you will be undertaking an iterative and simultaneous process that requires planning, adjusting, listening, and self-reflection. As you read ahead, the next chapters will provide an opportunity for qualitative data collection, and an examination of analysis strategies for both quantitative and qualitative approaches.

## 5.8 | Discussion

1. Qualitative research helps you gather perceptions and behavior around a particular topic. Describe a time when you have been an observer, participant, or collecting perceptions. Please expand on what the topic was and how it was or could have been used to inform decisions.
2. Circling back to Section 5.4, what do we (the authors) mean when we say, "Researchers must acknowledge their own positionality in the context of the research and the researched"?
3. Reflecting on what you learned in Section 5.5, a researcher's choice of categories when conducting content analysis is important. If the content analyses were focused on looking at School Site Council meeting minutes discussion about site-budget approvals, how would the choice of categories drive the research?
4. Think about qualitative research from a practitioner's perspective, what stakeholder voices are important and why should they be considered when writing school site plan, for example?
5. Again, think along the line of practical application and imagine two types of qualitative research methods (1) one-on-one interviews versus (2) focus groups. Now, provide an example where one method would be preferred over the other or an example where employing both methods would yield the most useful data?
6. Qualitative data can be more rigorous and time-consuming than quantitative research. Do you agree with this statement? Please explain your response while expanding on the benefits of both.

## 5.9 | Assignment: Qualitative Synthesis

This assignment introduces the next steps in your examination. As part of this assignment, you will begin to design your own data collection instruments informed by the quantitative data collected as part of Chapter 4 assignment. This next iteration of assignments will allow you to begin thinking about the qualitative aspects of your topic of interest. This assignment asks you to create protocols for primary data collection, for example, interview and for observation, and create a content analysis plan and identify several variables of interest.

> ### Template: Qualitative Synthesis
>
> [Please delete all directions and the instruction box below prior to submitting your Qualitative Synthesis assignment]
>
> ## Instructions
>
> This qualitative segment is your opportunity to take a deeper look at the scholarly literature and begin to construct qualitative protocols to examine equity concerns at your school site as documented in the quantitative data assignment (Chapter 4).
>
> This template will take place in two parts: (1) synthesis of the scholarly literature you annotated in as part of Chapter 3 assignment, and (2) create an interview protocol, observation protocol, and content analysis plan.
>
> The following components should be included in this assignment:
>
> - Synthesis of the annotated bibliography (a brief literature review)
> - Develop an interview protocol, observation protocol, and content analysis plan
>
> ## Synthesis
>
> As a starting point, take a look at the annotated bibliography and develop a short synthesis (a brief literature review) of the scholarly literature collected for Chapter 3; you should aim to include at least three to five sources in your synthesis. Particularly important will be to identify equity-related trends or patterns related to your topic of interest and population of focus.
>
> When drafting a synthesis of the literature, you should aim to construct two to three paragraphs of well-integrated writing (see Section 3.4). Identify equity-related trends or patterns related to your topic of interest/population of focus and highlight those. Use transition sentences to tie your paragraphs into a coherent and logical analysis of the literature you have collected.
>
> ## Interview Protocol
>
> Based on the quantitative data collection and synthesis (Chapter 4), here you are asked to design an interview protocol that will allow you to further explore your chosen topic and inform earlier quantitative findings. As discussed earlier, interviewing participants for your topic of interest is an important piece of the qualitative data collection puzzle. There exist plentiful examples of interviewing protocols on the internet, but the scripts generally include these sections:
>
> 1. **Logistical introduction.** This is where you explain the details of the procedures you will be following. Will you be taking notes? Recording? Did you obtain consent to interview? How long will this take? Explain confidentiality? and so on.
> 2. **Study introduction.** This section contains an explanation of what you are aiming to achieve by interviewing this person. Why did you select this interviewee? What is your research project about?
> 3. **Ask easier but engaging questions.** How long have you worked here? What is your role in the office? You can also build in probes where you want to get specific information from a question: How does the new policy limit your ability to interact with students? For richer information, ask open-ended questions—make revisions if necessary. Listen well and clarify or confirm statements.

4. **Ask more difficult and more specific questions.** To what extent are parents involved with after-school activities? How do you think you might better support your student teachers when they are learning how to reinforce goals in Individualized Educational Plans? Again, open-ended questions and probes will help you get the deep data you are seeking and will keep you on track.

5. **Demographic information.** These questions are important when you analyze your data. Again, it will be important as you position yourself in the context of this study.

6. **Closing.** Always show gratitude, even when the interview did not go as planned. Ask if the interviewee has any questions. You may also want to give them contact information if they have questions later or remembered something they want to be sure to tell you.

Authors Jacob and Ferguson (2012) have written a helpful article that is a great reference for more information on creating an interview protocol (Jacob & Furgerson, 2012).

### Observation Protocol

A very common type of qualitative data collection in education is a classroom observation (or a related educational setting). Some interventions in research come with detailed protocols on what to note, how to tally, or even when to use a clicker or timer. Protocols that are already validated have instructions on scoring and coding data to facilitate the use of a particular instrument. Of course, your observations may be quite different in nature. Perhaps you count how many times a teacher calls for quiet. Or watch how the younger students interact in a mixed classroom. If you are studying inequity, you may want to note interactions of a certain type in the student cafeteria.

As you can see, the observation protocol can look very different depending upon its purpose. Researchers who create their own instrument may need to revise as needed. Oftentimes, researchers test their instruments before officially fielding their study. Essentially, researchers create a systematic and standardized way to collect the information of interest as they conduct observations.

### Content Analysis Plan

As mentioned above, the idea behind this technique is to look at primary textual sources and create categories that are relevant to your research and count them. In education, these sources can be curriculum, books, essays, texts, emails, historical documents, meeting minutes, journal entries, blogs, board of supervisor agendas, and so on. You get the picture—as a researcher, you look for documents that are available—remember one important benefit of qualitative data, is to obtain a richer, deeper context for your topic of interest.

A content analysis plan may begin with expected "variables"—words, phrases, sentences, and possibly expected themes. A researcher can expect this plan to change as sources are reviewed and coded. "The process involves the simultaneous coding of raw data and the construction of categories that capture relevant characteristics of the document's content" (Merriam, 1998, p. 160).

## References

Birks, M., & Mills, J. (2012). *Grounded theory: A practical guide*. Sage.

Blackstone, A. (2012). *Principles of sociological inquiry: Qualitative and quantitative methods*. Saylor Foundation. https://doi.org/13:9781453328897

Campbell, M. (2018, July). Postmodernism and educational research. *Open Journal of Social Sciences, 6,* 67–73. https://doi.org/10.4236/jss.2018.67006.

Chun Tie, Y., Birks, M., & Francis, K. (2019). Grounded theory research: A design framework for novice researchers. *SAGE Open Medicine, 7,* 3. https://doi.org/10.1177/2050312118822927

Coghlan, D., & Brydon-Miller, M. (2014). *The SAGE encyclopedia of action research* (Vols. 1–2). SAGE Publications Limited. https://doi.org/10.4135/9781446294406

Corbin, J. M., & Anselm, S. (1990). Grounded theory research: Procedures, canons, and evaluative criteria. *Qualitative Sociology, 13(1),* 3–12. https://doi.org/10.1007/BF00988593

Fraenkel, J. R., Wallen, N. E., & Hyun, H. H. (2019). *How to design and evaluate research in education* (10th ed.). McGraw-Hill Education.

Glaser, B. G., & Strauss, A. (1967). *The discovery of grounded theory: Strategies for qualitative research.* Aldine Publishing Co.

Gustafsson, J. (2017). *Single case studies vs. multiple case studies: A comparative study (Thesis).* Halmstad University.

Jacob, S., & Furgerson, S. P. (2012). Writing interview protocols and conducting interviews: Tips for students new to the field of qualitative research. *The Qualitative Report, 17(6),* 1–10. http://www.nova.edu/ssss/QR/QR17/jacob.pdf

Kalekin-Fishman, D. (2002). Looking at interviewing: From "Just Talk" to meticulous method. *Forum: Qualitative Social Research, 3(4),* 17. http://nbn-resolving.de/urn:nbn:de:0114-fqs0204384

Merriam, S. B. (1998). *Qualitative research and case study applications in education.* Jossey-Bass.

Merriam, S. B., & Tisdell, E. J. (2016). *Qualitative research: A guide to design and implementation* (4th ed.). Jossey-Bass.

Monahan, T., & Fisher, J. A. (2010, June 1). Benefits of "observer effects": Lessons from the field. *Qualitative Research, 10(3),* 357–376. https://doi.org/10.1177/1468794110362874

Patel, L. (2016). *Decolonizing educational research: From ownership to answerability.* Routledge Publishing.

Thambinathan, V., & Kinsella, E. A. (2021). Decolonizing methodologies in qualitative research: Creating spaces for transformative praxis. *International Journal of Qualitative Methods, 20.* https://doi.org/10.1177%2F16094069211014766

Thorne, S. (2000). Data analysis in qualitative research. *Evidence Based Nursing, 3(3),* 68–70. https://doi.org/10.1136/ebn.3.3.68

Wilson, S. (1977). The use of ethnographic techniques in educational research. *Review of Educational Research, 47(1),* 245–265. https://www.cedu.niu.edu/~walker/research/Ethnographies%20Overall.pdf

Yazan, B. (2015). Three approaches to case study methods in education: Yin, Merriam, and Stake. *The Qualitative Report, 20(2),* 134–152. https://doi.org/10.46743/2160-3715/2015.2102

Yin, R. K. (2009). *Case study research: Design and methods* (4th ed.). Sage Publications.

# CHAPTER 6

# Mixed-methods Research and Application

*What are the effective ways to utilize qualitative and quantitative research to deepen understanding about school leadership and pedagogical practices?*

## 6.1 | Introduction

In prior chapters you learned about quantitative and qualitative research, as well as given an opportunity to apply your knowledge while learning these concepts. The goal of this chapter is to bring the prior learning together as we examine the mixed-methods approach to bridge your prior learning and assignments. In doing so, we first unpack the mixed-methods design. Then we discuss the effective ways that mixed-methods research design is used in education. Finally, we ask you to constructively think of ways to further inform your prior examination of quantitative data through the qualitative data collection assignment—as sequential examination employing mixed methods.

## 6.2 | Mixed-methods Research: An Overview

**Mixed-methods research is exactly what it sounds like—integrating or "mixing" of qualitative and quantitative methods.** Although it sounds simple, mixed-methods research design is quite purposeful and methodical in nature adhering to concrete steps and concepts. Originating in the social sciences, mixed-methods research gained much popularity in many hard sciences fields, such as health, medical sciences, social work, among many others. This said, however, the field of mixed-methods research is still considered emerging (spanning roughly over the last two decades or so), hence its procedures are continuously developed, revisited, and refined to suit a wide variety of research questions (Creswell & Clark, 2017).

The basic principle of this methodology is that the integration of both qualitative and quantitative methods affords a more complete, synorogenic analysis of data as compared to collecting and analyzing quantitative and qualitative data separately. Therefore, mixed-methods approach is particularly helpful when studying best practices since both deductive (quantitative) and inductive (qualitative) as well as the examination of interactions of these data are necessary to evaluate practice and make practice-related change as a result of this evaluation. To give you a better sense of how mixed-methods research is used as a tool in practice, in Figure 6.1, we provide a narrative unpacking a problem and employment a mixed-methods design approach.

> **Freshbite Challenge: Mixed-methods Study to the Rescue**
>
> Freshbite is a one-and-half-year-old e-commerce start-up company delivering fresh foods as per the order to customer's doorstep through its delivery partners. The company operates in multiple cities.
>
> Since its inception, the company achieved a high sales growth rate. However, after completion of the first year, **the sales started declining at brisk rate**. Due to lack of historical data, the sales director was confused about **the reasons for this decline in sales**. He selected to appoint a **marketing research consultant to conduct an exploratory research study** in order to discern the possible reasons rather than making assumptions.
>
> **The prime objective** of this research was not to figure out a solution to the declining sales problem, but rather **to identify the possible reasons**, such as poor quality of products and services, competition, or ineffective marketing, **and to better understand the factors affecting sales**. Once these potential causes are identified, **then the strength of each reason can be tested using causal research.**

**Figure 6.1:** Example of Mixed-methods Research Applied in Practice
Adapted from https://www.smstudy.com/article/exploratory-research-design

> **Exercise** With one other peer or in a small group, read and discuss the narrative in Figure 6.1. Then, based on the description, draft what might go into the research proposal to execute this study, that is, what might be the topic, research question(s), and steps for the mixed-methods research design? For example, what type of research method (i.e., qualitative/quantitative) was utilized in the first and second data collection and analysis steps? And how were the data potentially analyzed in the end? HINT: Pay attention to the bolded text and think about each step as an integral part of the analysis.

As we are about to dive into unpacking the most commonly used mixed-methods designs in education, we would like to note that the use of mixed methods must be purposeful and systematic. That is, it is not simply enough to engage in quantitative and qualitative research and call it a mixed-methods study. A mixed-methods design must be considered and consulted throughout the study, prior, during, and in the last stages of final interpretation. In Section 6.3, we outline four helpful questions for a researcher/researcher practitioner to consider while planning a mixed-methods research study.

## 6.3 | Mixed-method Research Approaches and Designs in Education: Sequential and Concurrent

In general, there are two types of mixed-methods approaches that are most commonly used in the field of education: sequential and concurrent. These approaches morph into more specific designs that give precedence to either qualitative or quantitative method. We unpack the most frequently used below.

### Sequential Approach

Sequential designs in mixed-methods research adhere to a linear structure, a sequence of steps where the initial step of data collection and analysis informs the next integration of data collection/analysis resulting in final interpretation of findings. In the field of education, the two sequential designs that are most commonly used are explanatory and exploratory.

## Chapter 6: Mixed-methods Research and Application

**Sequential Explanatory Design.** The purpose of explanatory design is to use qualitative results to help explain and further interpret quantitative findings. This design is characterized by the first leg in the sequence: quantitative data collection and analysis, followed by the second leg in the sequence: qualitative data collection and analysis, where the quantitative segment is central to the study by providing a general picture of the research problem, followed by the qualitative segment to further explain, inform, or extend quantitative findings.

**Table 6.1:** Sequential Explanatory Design Conceptual Representation

| QUANT → *follow up with* | qual → | Final Interpretation |
|---|---|---|
| Guided by quantitative question(s), data collection, and analysis—*quantitative data component is central to the research study* | Guided by qualitative question(s), data collection, and analysis *to help explain or further interpret quantitative results* | Based on the quantitative findings (primary) and qualitative interpretation (secondary) |

Examples of studies utilizing the sequential explanatory design include:

- School Culture Study: School Climate Survey (numerical/closed-ended)—first and primary leg in the sequence provides a general picture through quantitative results and *followed up with* staff interviews (qualitative/opened-ended)—second leg in the sequence
- Academic Performance Equity Gap: Mathematics standardized achievement data for English learner and English-only middle school students (numerical/closed-ended)—first and primary leg in the sequence provides a general picture through quantitative results and *followed up with* teacher interviews, observations of instruction, and content analysis of documents (qualitative/opened-ended)—second leg in the sequence.

**Sequential Exploratory Design.** The purpose of the exploratory design is to explore a phenomenon or test a new instrument. This design is characterized by the first leg in the sequence: qualitative data collection and analysis, followed by the second leg in the sequence: quantitative data collection and analysis. Where qualitative segment is central to the study and is used to explore a phenomenon first followed by a quantitative data collection and analysis to explain relationships found in the qualitative data (see Table 6.2). In the larger scale studies, the quantitative segment (e.g., a survey) builds on the qualitative findings to provide generalizability and, therefore, the qualitative segment of the study frames the quantitative segment (see second examples).

**Table 6.2:** Sequential Exploratory Design Conceptual Representation

| QUAL → *builds to* | quant → | Final Interpretation |
|---|---|---|
| Guided by qualitative question(s), data collection, and analysis—*qualitative data component is central to the research study* | Guided by quantitative question(s), data collection, and analysis *to help explain relationships found in qualitative data* | Based on the qualitative findings (primary) and quantitative interpretation (secondary) |

Examples of studies utilizing the sequential explanatory design include:

- Education Community Needs Study: Focus groups with a representative sample of teachers, staff, and parents (qualitative/opened-ended)—the first and primary leg in the sequence to explore school site needs—after data collection and analysis, the findings then *build to* and help inform a quantitative survey (numerical/closed-ended) to concretely identify priority needs—second leg in the sequence.

- New-To-the-Profession Teacher Challenges: A series of interviews with new to the profession teachers who have been in the profession for three or less years (qualitative/opened-ended)—the first and primary leg in the sequence to explore teachers' experiences and expectations—these interview findings *build to* and helped inform a large-scale online quantitative survey that included thousands of participants.

**Sequential Transformative Design.** A sequential transformative design adheres to the same conceptual principles of the sequential approach as the explanatory and exploratory designs (see Tables 6.1 and 6.2). What is different, however, is that a study engaging transformative design is guided by a theory or theoretical underpinnings. The purpose of this design is to employ the methods to best serve a theoretical perspective.

## Concurrent Approach

The concurrent mixed-method design allows the qualitative and quantitative data collection and analysis occur at the same time or in parallel to one another.

**Concurrent Triangulation Design.** The purpose of this design is to validate the findings generated by each method. Concurrent triangulation design involves a study encompassing qualitative and quantitative data collection and analysis that are conducted around the same time to answer a single research question. Generally, both qualitative and quantitative data collections and analyses carry equal in concurrent triangulation mixed-method design. The purpose of the interpretive stage of the design is to cross validate qualitative and quantitative findings and obtain different but complementary data (see Table 6.3).

Table 6.3: Concurrent Triangulation Design Conceptual Representation

| Qual → | Interpretation | ← Quant |
|---|---|---|
| Guided by qualitative question(s), data collection, and analysis—*qualitative data component is equal or given more weight (based on the project and goals of the study) to the quantitative component, analyzed separately* | The interpretation of different but complementary data in the concurrent triangulation design is used to cross validate qualitative and quantitative findings | Guided by quantitative question(s), data collection, and analysis—*quantitative data component is equal to the qualitative component or given more weight (based on the project and goals of the study), analyzed separately* |

Examples of studies utilizing the concurrent triangulation design include:

- High School Jr. Parental Knowledge of College Readiness Study: Focus group discussions and individual interviews with parents of high school juniors (qualitative/opened-ended) affording an examination into parental knowledge about college readiness conducted simultaneously with the gathering of quantitative college readiness data collection, for example, types of courses taken or lacking, progress toward high school exit exam completion, college entry exam data, and so on (numerical/closed-ended) to cross validate qualitative and quantitative findings, that is, parental understanding of their perceptions about college readiness and their students' actual college readiness
- Parental School Satisfaction: Mailed satisfaction survey to all parents in the school district (numerical/closed-ended) while undertook unstructured interviews with a representative sample of parents from each school site (qualitative/opened-ended) to cross validate qualitative and quantitative findings.

**Concurrent Nested Design.** The purpose of the concurrent nested design is to answer a complementary research question by obtaining different data sources. Although both qualitative and quantitative data are being collected simultaneously, in concurrent nested mixed-methods research studies, one method (either qualitative or quantitative) dominates, and the other is nested within the dominant method (see Figure 6.2). Therefore, the question posed by the dominant method is the central question of the study. On the other hand, the embedded question is either secondary or very specific to the nested subtopic. Consequently, the embedded method and data collection are designed to be complementary.

**Figure 6.2:** Conceptual Representation of Concurrent Nested Design

- Performance Curriculum Impact on English Learners Study: A 3-month long randomized control trial to study the impact of performance curriculum on the language acquisition among English learners by incorporating themes from students' home culture as compared to traditional methods of teaching. Pre- and post-study tests (numerical/closed-ended) to measure language acquisition outcomes of exposing students to such curriculum/method of teaching with a nested observation and unstructured interviews component (qualitative/opened-ended) during the course of study to examine the process and better understand social wellbeing impact on the students.

**Concurrent Transformative Design.** A concurrent transformative design adheres to the same conceptual principles of the concurrent approach as the triangulation and nested designs (see Table 6.3 and Figure 6.2). What is different, is that a study engaging transformative design is guided by a theory or theoretical underpinnings. The purpose of this design is to evaluate a theoretical perspective at different levels of analysis. Therefore, and similar to sequential transformative design, all mixed-methods designs that are guided by theoretical underpinnings are commonly referred to as transformative designs.

## 6.4 | Planning Mixed-method Research

As you plan a mixed-methods study, remember that the field of mixed methods is relatively new, dynamic, and continues to expand. There are many more mixed-methods research designs than we could possibly cover in a chapter. In the previous section, we unpacked the most commonly used mixed-methods approaches and designs in the field of education. Here, we outline a number of tips to help you conceptualize and navigate the initial stages of a mixed-methods study.

When considering a mixed-methods design approach, it is important to grasp the terms and nature of mixed methods as having two distinct methodological components. Likewise, it is equally important to differentiate between what does and does not represent a mixed-methods research design. There are, for example, studies that employ both methods but would not be considered mixed methods. Survey research (see Chapter 10) is one of these examples. That is, many survey studies employ both quantitative/numerical closed-ended scales and qualitative questions in an open-ended format in one survey, the design is not considered to be mixed methods; the research is a survey study aiming at gathering participants' insights by qualitative and quantitative means.

What makes mixed-methods design unique is the interwoven nature of both methods and the interdependence of these methods on one another in answering the central research question of a study. Put differently, in order for a research study to be considered a mixed-methods study, there must be an authentic and systemic "integration of the data at one or more stages in the process of research" (Creswell et al., 2003, p. 212).

Accordingly, as you plan your mixed-methods research study, Creswell (2003) suggested to first consider the following four questions:

1. In what *sequence* will the qualitative and quantitative data collection be implemented? [Determining the sequence for a sequential approach (or determining the lack thereof) will help guide you in the right direction of selecting appropriate design for the study]
2. What relative *priority* will be given to the qualitative and quantitative data collection and analysis? [Knowing the priority of the method to be used will help in narrowing down the design to be used]
3. *At what stage* of the project will *the qualitative and quantitative data be integrated*? [By determining when the methods are intergraded will help you narrow down/solidify both the approach and design of research study]
4. Will an overall *theoretical perspective* be used to guide the study? [Answering this question will help you determine whether a transformative design will be employed/necessary]

While reviewing the above questions, notice the key terms: sequence, priority, integration, and the use of a theoretical perspective are all critical to consider when narrowing down which mixed-methods design is the most applicable and best suited for your study.

It should also be noted that mixed-methods sequential and concurrent approaches and their corresponding designs are regularly used in review and evaluation as more than one method is necessary in an evaluative assessment to overcome limitations of a single method. One of the examples would be the application engagements and assignments that we asked you to partake in the prior chapters. We continue this discussion below.

## 6.5 | Application

*What are the effective ways to utilize mixed methods to deepen understanding about school leadership and pedagogical practices?*

As you were learning about mixed methods, you probably recognized that previous application engagements and assignments from earlier chapters led you on a mixed-methods examination path. This was intentionally done. Our goal was to provide you with an opportunity to explore how different methods are applied independently as we unpacked qualitative and quantitative methods, and now is the time to unpack how they would interact together in a more structured, sequential, and purposeful approach. Let us first review prior engagements. Through application sections and assignments, you were asked to

- Chapter 2: (1) examine state indicators (i.e., state's priorities) for data collection and tracking, (2) select an indicator in light of a familiar school context by examining school site data, (3) identify a topic and draft a research question(s) as part of the Plan of Action Part I Assignment
- Chapter 3: (4) find and annotate scholarly literature to further inform your topic and research questions, (5) review and potentially revise your chosen topic/research question(s) as you expanded your knowledge on the topic as part of the Plan of Action Part II Assignment
- Chapter 4: (6) find, document, and review longitudinal trends of quantitative data as part of Quantitative Data Exercise and Synthesis Assignment
- Chapter 5: (7) design a qualitative protocol aligned with your topic/research questions with the goal of gathering qualitative data from three different sources

# Chapter 6: Mixed-methods Research and Application

> **QUESTION** Alone or with a peer, review the assignments that you completed thus far with the help of the list above. After your review and based on your newly acquired knowledge about mixed-methods research (see Section 6.3), determine which mixed-method design you are following. Explain how you narrowed down your answer.

Before we continue on a path of deepening our knowledge about using research as a tool on the subject of mixed methods, we would like to pause and review the significance of data in the field of Education. The vast majority of you were asked to rely on or at least heard about data-driven instruction or data-driven decision-making or evidence-based practices, among other like terms. Notice the words "data" and "evidence" as central qualifiers for all these terms. It is generally agreed upon across fields that we need evidence to engage in an informed practice. The field of education is no exception. And, for us to have evidence, we must gather and examine data. Therefore, we argue that engaging in informed practice is simply impossible without data, especially when reform or a change in educational processes is necessary. Accordingly, it is imperative to know what data you need, where to find and/or how to collect these data.

Mixed-methods research design provides a template for a more comprehensive examination since it allows for the purposeful integration of qualitative and quantitative data. In the previous chapters, we talked about and had you engage in a review of published (e.g., research articles) or reported data (e.g., school site reports, or data included in a repository, such as CDE's EdData)—both are necessary to draw conclusions in practice or research and serve as building blocks for one another in establishing evidence. This said, however, the picture would not be complete without a qualitative inquiry into understanding the potential "why" related to the specific context of the school site. The process involves understanding the field through the works of others, examining specific quantitative data about a population of focus in any given school context, and then informing the quantitative evidence by gathering qualitative data to understand the "why." In others words, following the sequential explanatory design steps (see Table 6.1: QUANT qual), which is one of the most commonly utilized methods in education.

Suppose you were to take a closer look; you will quickly recognize that the explanatory design is often used in school reports and encouraged by school leaders to evaluate pedagogical practice. Put differently, to understand academic achievement within the unique context of a classroom, program/department, or school site, it is necessary to examine quantitative data as a fundamental step followed by a qualitative examination in order to sufficiently engage in a thorough analysis of the existing gaps and issues. Without such an examination, it would be impossible to identify an equity gap or a problem of practice to take further action toward improvement. Thus, these steps are essential for data-driven practices to take root in educational settings.

In this segment of applying your knowledge, we suggest that you connect with your peer-review group[1] (or, alternatively, work independently) and **circle back to your prior completed assignments**, specifically to your Plan of Action assignments, quantitative data exercise from Chapter 4 and the qualitative protocol assignment from Chapter 5. Once you do, review the quantitative data synopsis (Chapter 4 assignment), think about and discuss the specific context of your site and **identify *three* qualitative sources that would help inform your quantitative findings**. These **qualitative sources need to be primary** (meaning first account).

One example of a qualitative source could be *people* (e.g., interviews with teachers and/or administrators at the school site, focus group discussion, and/or interviews/conversation accounts with students and parents). Another example is *observations* (e.g., your own observation(s) of classroom practices or observations of school site-specific dynamics, etc.). And yet, another example of a qualitative source could constitute

---

[1] Your peer review group was created in Chapter 3 and designed to connect two-three people with liked interests.

*documents* (e.g., content analysis of school site documents, reports, departmental pacing guides, other schoolwide plans, etc.). As you think about and identify your qualitative sources, we ask that you consult your topic and quantitative data—remember, research is a process where everything is purposefully connected, especially when using a mixed-method approach. The goal here is to further inform your quantitative findings through several qualitative means. Next, when you think about your three sources of qualitative data, the three sources could be a combination of one interview, one observation, and one content analysis of site documents, OR two interviews (e.g., one with a teacher and another with an administrator) and one observation, OR one interview, and two observations, and so on. What is important is that you need three total and to try out at least two qualitative modalities.

Once you identify the data sources, adjust the qualitative protocol from Chapter 5 accordingly[2] in preparation for qualitative data collection.

## 6.6 | Conclusion

We hope this chapter unpacked the exciting world of mixed-methods design and helped bring the prior assignments together in a cohesive way. As discussed in the application section, the mixed-methods approach is one of the most common approaches utilized in education. More than one method is often necessary to fully grasp the existing equity gaps within the educational systems as these relate to student academic achievement and/or well-being. This chapter is also uniquely positioned to bring the many prior building blocks together and engage you in the primary data collection assignment to inform your earlier quantitative findings further—an intentional process of immersing you in research activities to tryout and solidify your learned research skills through the practical application as you gain knowledge. We hope that this chapter gave you one more tool/a skill set to navigate the data and evidence in the field of education.

## 6.7 | Discussion

1. Now that you learned about mixed methods, what do you see as the value of integrating quantitative and qualitative methods in educational research/as you apply these in practice?
2. Describe a report or project that you engaged in at your school site where the leadership or a community of educators illustrated quantitative and qualitative data and/or results of these data?
3. Reflecting on your current role at the school site, describe a problem of practice within your classroom (or other) setting where gathering quantitative and qualitative data would help you improve instruction?
4. School site plans are submitted annually, what measures (quantitative and qualitative) help leadership teams with school planning?
5. In your own words, define mixed-methods research and cite a research question that justifies its use?

## 6.8 | Assignment: Qualitative Data Collection

This assignment is a continuation of the application section (Section 6.5). In the application section, you were asked to identify three sources of primary qualitative data and adjust qualitative protocols accordingly.

---

2 Only use applicable protocols—do note, if you are conducting two interviews with different people, you might want to adjust your interview protocol to align with the interviewee's role.

The next step is to engage in qualitative data collection from the identified three qualitative sources with. Before you start data collection, please review the following:

1. Make sure that the **qualitative protocols and data collection** that you are about to embark on are **aligned with your topic and designed to expand/inform your understandings on the identified issue/equity gap found as part of your school site quantitative longitudinal data investigation**
2. **Identify the most appropriate qualitative sources to further inform your quantitative findings**, for example, either people (teachers, administrators, parents, students, and so on) or by means of your own observations, or through content analysis of school site documents (for more information, see Section 6.5)
3. Be ready to **collect three sources of data, by utilizing at least two qualitative modalities**. For example: (1) **a focus group interview** with math teachers who teach English learners, (2) **an interview with a school site administrator** to gain insights into measures to close the academic performance equity gap on mathematics between English learners and their English-only counterparts, and (3) **content analysis of professional development meeting documents** focusing on English learner academic achievement.

Depending on your selection of the three qualitative sources, your final assignment must include a transcript of your interview(s), observation notes, and/or review of documents. These are necessary in order to continue with data analysis as outlined in the next chapter.

# References

Creswell, J. W., & Plano Clark, V. L. (2017). *Designing and conducting mixed methods research* (3rd ed.). SAGE Publications.

Creswell, J. W, Plano Clark, V., Gutmann, M., and Hanson, W. (2003). Advanced mixed methods research designs. In A. Tashakkori and C Teddle (Eds.), *Handbook of mixed methods in social and behavioral research* (pp. 212). Thousand Oaks, CA : Sage.

Creswell, J. W. (2003). Research design: Qualitative, quantitative, and mixed methods approaches (2nd ed.). Thousand Oaks, CA: Sage.

**CHAPTER 7**

# Data Fluency: The Foundations of Quantitative and Qualitative Data Analysis

*Now that I completed data collection, what do I do?*

## 7.1 | Introduction

Depending on your current career or standing in the field of Education, you may or may not be crunching numbers or working with qualitative data to come to valid conclusions, yet it is critical to have a basic understanding of the data you are reviewing. This basic understanding of what data are showing is sometimes called "data literacy." As you progress through and engage in the activities outlined in this text, you are exposed to enough information to point you toward "data fluency." Our goal for this text all along has been to expose educators to enough information and hands-on experiential learning to ensure that educators, administrators, and school leaders achieve enough data fluency to make evidence-based decisions.

The first part of this chapter introduces some basic concepts in quantitative data analysis, with the second part exploring basic processes for qualitative data analysis. The purpose of this chapter is to help answer the question, *"Now that I have completed data collection, what do I do?"* Of course, it bears mentioning that education researchers spend entire careers dealing with these topics; therefore, it is important to understand that the information presented in this chapter is foundational to get you started on the path of using research as a tool.

As we work to unpack data **analysis** in this chapter, we will progress in the same order as earlier in the text. First, we discuss quantitative data analysis. We then review the essential elements of qualitative data analysis. Finally, we ask you to examine how the qualitative analysis segment helped deepen your understanding of your quantitative findings.

## 7.2 | Toward Understanding Your Quantitative Data

### Descriptive Statistics

You first encountered the term "descriptive statistics" in Chapter 2 of this textbook. In Chapter 4, you were asked to gather quantitative data related to your topic/population of focus for three different sources, the main being the school site you identified earlier. You were also asked to write a short synopsis of your findings. In this section, we will take a deeper look at the types of descriptive statistics and which type might best suit your data. Descriptive statistics is an umbrella term that can include a variety of methods to display and describe quantitative data. (They are also used in qualitative data in a bit of a different way—this will be discussed in Section 7.3 of this chapter).

> Analysis is a detailed examination
>
> Data Analysis is the process of systematically applying statistical and/or logical techniques to describe and illustrate, condense and recap, and evaluate data.

Researchers, researcher-practitioners, and study authors use descriptive data specifically to describe the basic features and elements of data collected in a study. Descriptive data might oftentimes include multiple depictions of data, or even data broken down into summaries. It is certainly true that any quantitative studies may describe the sample, frequencies, and even measures of central tendencies. Let us take a look at some typical descriptive statistics used in describing a study sample.

## *Frequencies*

When researchers describe their study sample, they demonstrate how representative the sample might be to the general population of interest. How many subjects ended up in the same category? How were test scores distributed? How many students answered in a particular way? It is important to remember that descriptive statistics simply "describe" data—no inferences or conclusions are made.

Figure 7.5 "Student Sample Characteristics" in Chapter 2 is a good example of a descriptive table—it shows frequencies of sample demographics and corresponding percentages. These frequencies alone can provide insight into any particular quantitative study. In Table 7.1, we provide another example of a frequency distribution table. This data comes from a state sample of California students answering the California Healthy Kids Survey between 2015 and 2017. This table uses percentages, but is still considered a "frequency table." As you review the data, you will notice many changes in self-reported truancy as students get older. By the time students reach Grade 11 in California, you can see that between 7% and 8% of them miss school at least once per week. Simply describing these data gives you a meaningful understanding of the extent of truancy in California. Furthermore, it gives the reader an important look as to how the data are distributed across the various grade levels. This concept of distribution is another important feature of descriptive statistics.

**Table 7.1:** Self-Reported Truancy in California in Last 12 Months

*Truancy, Past 12 Months*

|  | Grade 7 | | Grade 9 | | Grade 11 | |
| --- | --- | --- | --- | --- | --- | --- |
|  | 2013–2015 (%) | 2015–2017 (%) | 2013–2015 (%) | 2015–2017 (%) | 2013–2015 (%) | 2015–2017 (%) |
| 0 times | 70.3 | 74.3 | 65.1 | 66.8 | 50.3 | 54.5 |
| 1–2 times | 14.8 | 13.3 | 15.5 | 15.1 | 18.3 | 17.7 |
| A few times | 11.3 | 9.8 | 12.6 | 12.5 | 19.0 | 17.7 |
| Once a month | 1.2 | 1.1 | 2.0 | 1.7 | 4.4 | 3.1 |
| Once a week | 0.7 | 0.5 | 1.4 | 1.2 | 3.2 | 2.8 |
| More than once a week | 1.6 | 0.9 | 3.3 | 2.8 | 4.8 | 4.1 |

*Question HS/MS A.19: During the past 12 months, about how many times did you skip school or cut classes?*
**Source:** (Austin et al., 2018)

## *Measures of Central Tendency*

As researchers begin to analyze their data, another insightful descriptions are measures of central tendency, which are also known as "averages." Table 7.2 describes the three most commonly used averages which succinctly lets researchers know where the data are tending toward. In the end, while averages can tell researchers where "most" of the data are pooling, intuitively, we know that not all averages are created equal—that is, the context of the rest of the collected data is also an important element in understanding data.

# Chapter 7: Data Fluency: The Foundations of Quantitative and Qualitative Data Analysis

**Table 7.2:** Measures of Central Tendency

| Type of Average | Definition | Example | When to use | Danger |
|---|---|---|---|---|
| Mean | The sum of scores or numbers divided by the amount of numbers. | The mean score on the reading comprehension test was 78%. | When establishing average performance and which students might be above or below the average. This is the preferred measure of central tendency in Education Research. | Does not a give good idea of extreme or outlying scores. Can hide real picture of data tendency. |
| Mode | The number that appears most often. | The most frequently obtained score on the reading comprehension test was 81%. | Not used much in education research. | Simply identifying the most frequently occurring score does not provide much insight. Especially when you realize there might be two modes in one dataset. |
| Median | The middle number when numbers are placed in ascending order. | The median score on the reading comprehension test was 72%. | When the data are part of a skewed distribution the median shows the exact point where 50% of the data fall below or above the score. | Cannot be used for further analysis because it does not consider actual numeric values. Rather, it simply shows the middle value. |

## *Variance*

Researchers can think of variance as the "context" of data; that is, certain data points exist amidst a bigger data picture. The mean score on a test might be 78% but that alone does not give a complete data picture. Figure 7.1 displays two data curves; they are both considered normal curves—meaning that the center of the curve is the average data point and that the data points above or below the center are evenly distributed (symmetrical). The story told in Figure 7.2 is that the distribution of data may be tightly distributed, as in Curve A or widely distributed, as in Curve B.

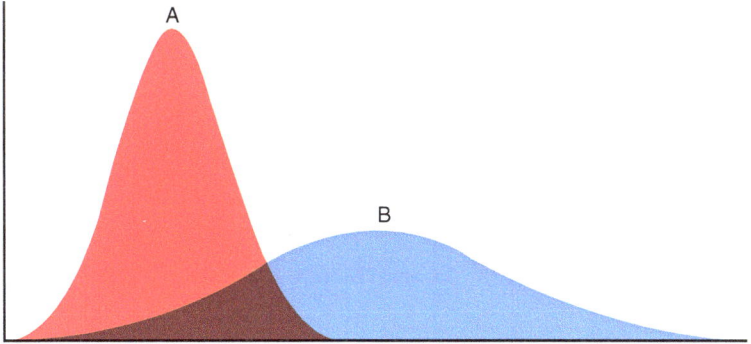

**Figure 7.1:** Normal Curves With Different Data Ranges

In a skewed distribution, data points are not normally distributed but cluster more on one side than the other (not symmetrical). Figure 7.2 shows us the Household Income distribution for the fictional school district of Palo Roto. You can see that most families in this school district report lower income categories. It is not essential that you look at the actual categories to understand that the average income for most households is on the lower end of the range. The type of skewed distribution is also called "positively skewed" or "right-skewed" because the data "tail" extends further to the right than it would in a normal distribution. You will notice that Figure 7.3 is also skewed, but in the opposite direction. As you might assume, this type of distribution is referred to as "negatively skewed" or "left-skewed."

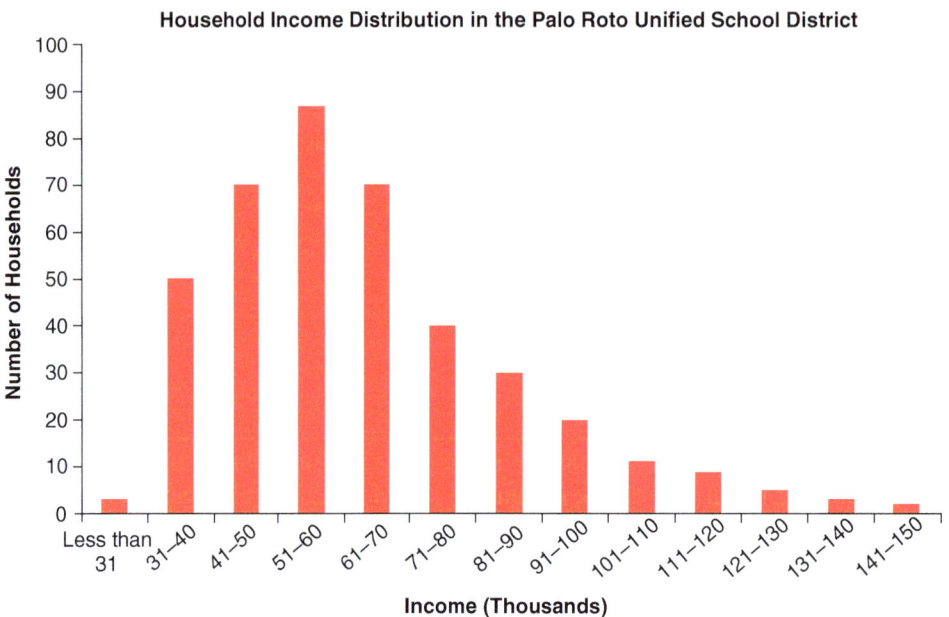

**Figure 7.2:** Positively Skewed Distribution Example

© Marta del Valle Induni

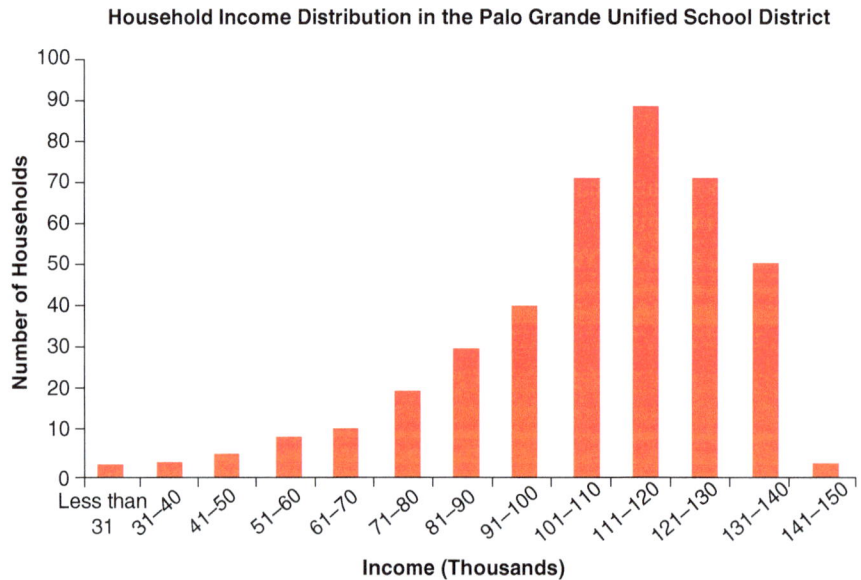

**Figure 7.3:** Negatively Skewed Distribution Example

© Marta del Valle Induni

## Measures of Relationship

Although less evident, "Measures of Relationship" can also be considered as descriptive data. Thus far, the text has explained descriptive statistics for one variable (univariate). As the word "relationship" implies, however, there are two frequently used descriptions: correlations and regressions.

**Correlations.** In technical terms, a correlation demonstrates the interaction of two variables on an $x$, $y$ axis. A correlation is said to be positive when the values of $x$ increase as the values of $x$ increase. If one value increases as the other decreases, it is said to be a negative correlation. The scatter diagrams below provide good examples of the linear relationships between two variables. When looking at correlations, there is no firm suggestion regarding which variable is mapped on the $x$-axis and which on the $y$-axis. After all, you will discover either a positive correlation, no correlation, or a negative correlation. Figure 7.4 gives a good depiction of the direction of the correlation and the strength of it. As might be evident in Figure 7.4, correlations are measured between positive one or negative one, with zero indicating no relationship between the two variables.

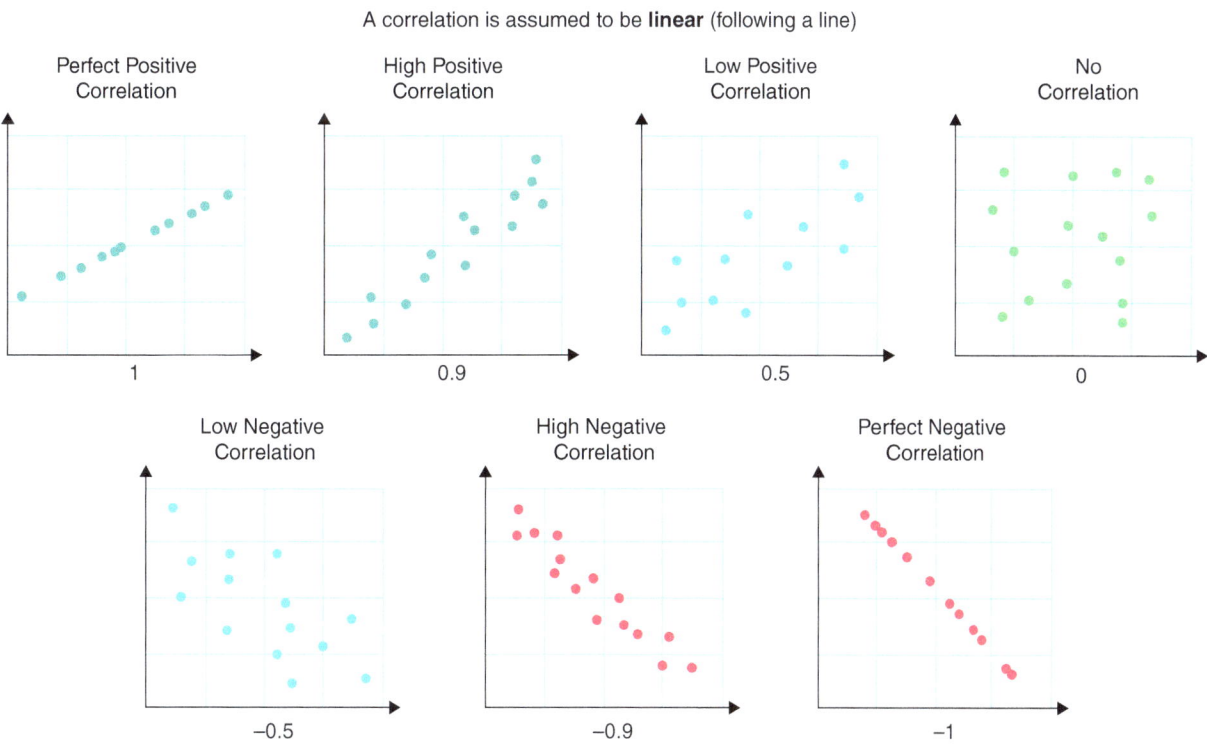

Figure 7.4: Correlation Scatter Plots and Strength of Relationship

Most discussions around correlation will be careful to warn the reader that "correlation does not imply causation." All we are mapping is the direction of the value of one variable in relation to another variable — we are not indicating that one variable causes the value of the second variable. There are many examples on the Internet that demonstrate this important caveat—researchers call these "spurious correlations." An example would be the near perfect positive correlation between mozzarella cheese consumption and civil engineering doctorates awarded in the United States.

**Regressions.** Correlations describe the strength of a relationship between two variables, whereas the purpose of regression is to predict and explain relationships, thus serving as a direct entry to inferential statistics and data modeling. A regression analysis will include an independent and dependent variable on each axis.

One final note, as the purpose of this section is to state descriptive statistics in plain terms, many studies will include analyses of multiple variables: multiple-correlation or multiple-regression examinations. Furthermore, another type of descriptive data can be seen in Figure 7.5. Mapping data onto geographic spaces is an effective way of communicating frequencies, distributions, and correlations in one tableau.

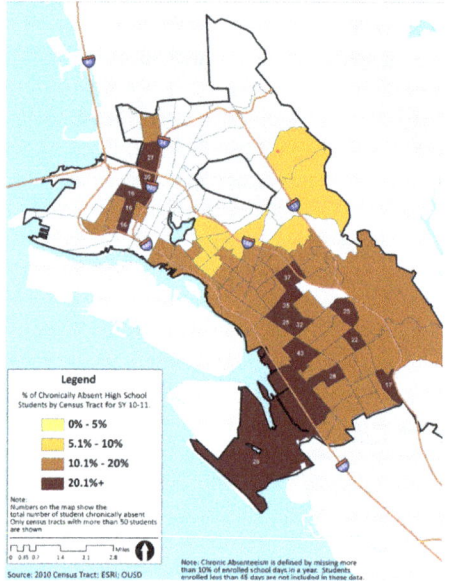

**Figure 7.5:** Percent of Chronically Absent High School Students by Oakland Census Tract, School Year 2010–2012

Source: (ESRI, 2014)

## 7.3 | Toward Understanding Your Qualitative Data

### Descriptive Statistics

Although much less quantitative in nature, it is important to describe your sample whenever you are analyzing your qualitative data. Researchers undertake this practice to describe the subjects of interest, the interviewees, the primary sources in a content review, or particular methods used that are self-reflexive. As was discussed in Chapter 5, qualitative data is a valuable method for anything that cannot be observed; such as deep and rich philosophies of interviewees, motivations of your subjects of interest, contexts that place the researcher into the research itself.

### Data Hygiene

Another important aspect of qualitative research is that the process of data collection and analysis typically happens concurrently. In effect, a researcher plans their data collection methods, data collection materials

# Chapter 7: Data Fluency: The Foundations of Quantitative and Qualitative Data Analysis

(charts, tally lists, checklists, and so on). However, those plans are under constant revision as the data collection progresses. A qualitative interview may start with a particular question and the participant may take it to an entirely different and unexpected direction. An astute researcher will incorporate this new finding or new direction into subsequent interviews and ultimately into their analyses. A careful researcher will review, refine, and edit data throughout the data collection process and throughout the analysis phase also. This process is critical as qualitative researchers seek to uncover theories or phenomenon through the act of research itself (Thorne, 2000).

## Qualitative Approaches

There are many standard practices used to analyze qualitative data. In addition to keeping data organized and aligned with a particular methodology, qualitative researchers will include annotations across their data: these could include the beginnings of coding structures and categories, reflections, thoughts on their own positionality and context, spotting patterns, looking for generalizations, and perhaps unveiling more formalized constructs or theories that fit the data (Lester et al., 2020).

As with quantitative analysis, qualitative researchers should strive to create a transparent and replicable methodology regarding their data collection and iterative analysis techniques. Augmenting the notion of self-reflection in one's qualitative work, Yin (2013) suggests a rigorous examination of the methodologies chosen for a particular qualitative study and the resulting outcomes.

## Qualitative Data Coding

*So, now that you collected qualitative data, what is next?* Once an interview, a focus group discussion, or an observation is complete, you must transcribe these data to ensure that there is an account of **"raw" data**. A transcription of an interview or observation account is necessary to progress to the next stage, coding. If you are about to engage in content analysis of a text, then often no transcription is necessary since the text is already transcribed in print and available in a form (preferably electronic) that could be coded.

**Coding** of qualitative data is the next step after transcription of an interview or a focus group discussion, or as you embark on an examination/content analysis of a primary text. The basic definition of qualitative data coding is "a way of indexing or categorizing the text in order to establish a framework of thematic ideas about it" (Gibbs, 2007). Coding is essential in qualitative research to be able to define what qualitative data are all about in a consistent, structured manner. Similar to other steps in research, *coding is a process* that starts with a broader interpretation or labeling (e.g., **open coding**, see Figure 7.6), followed by narrowing or combining the initial labels, and finally determining the final code or theme. Figure 7.7, illustrates these stages in the coding process. Likewise, often researchers add memos for themselves to keep track of important observations to help guide next steps in the coding process—Figure 7.6 includes an example of a coding memo. As you engage in and proceed with qualitative data coding, what is important to remember is that no matter how scrupulous you are as you code, the main goal of coding is to "open-up the text and expose the meaning, idea, and thoughts in it" (Khandkar, n.d., p.1) to be able to build concepts and derive conclusions from a textual source of raw data.

---

> Raw data can also be considered as noncleaned or nontransformed data. For qualitative coding, it refers to transcripts that are not coded or parsed—a verbatim record of data.

> Coding: "Coding in qualitative inquiry is defined as a word or short phrased that are central to the open narrative/answer given by a participant or as related to a question related to the topic/research question(s) of the study/investigation. Same application is relevant in the content analysis where the code is a word or a phrase in the text that provides insight into a topic/question(s) of the study."

> Open Coding: "In the process of Open Coding, the concepts emerge from the raw data and later grouped into conceptual categories. The goal is to build a descriptive, multi-dimensional preliminary framework for later analysis. As its build directly from the raw data, it process itself ensures the validity of the work."
>
> http://pages.cpsc.ucalgary.ca/~saul/wiki/uploads/CPSC681/open-coding.pdf

| Mc_Interview 1_23/4/20XX (58 mins) ||
|---|---|
| **Interview Transcript** | **Open Coding** |
| *I: In comparison to what you are doing now, do you think things are getting more systematic, or complicated?*<br>T: Well, I can't say that it is getting more complicated. It is getting more organized and clearer. More things are now written with specifications, for both my colleagues and myself. For example, as I am now the activities supervisor, I have produced a work schedule for the year, which could be passed on to my successor. This is in regards to administrative work. On the planning side for our own subject, says P.E., we have not specified the work to be done on monthly basis, but we have planned by projects or schemes. For example, say we had a "little athletes" scheme; we would have written a proposal for the whole plan, which my colleagues and I would follow.<br>*I: So, you mean you did not have a job description; nevertheless you have developed your job to a stage where things are getting more systematic and mature and even have some automated processes. Can these processes be regarded as a kind of operation manual which you can pass on to your successors?*<br>T: Yes. But this does not apply to everything. Particularly, in my curriculum development work I have not developed things to such a level yet. Changes are still on their way as things are still in an initial phase. There were hardly any standard procedures. | —Accepts the culture, values, and attitudes of the members in the organization.<br>—Internal quality of teaching as a profession<br>—Assimilates a web of values based on a social consensus of professional behavior—indirect learning.<br>—Accepts and behaves in ways that are appropriate to that organization.<br>—Acts independently.<br>—Commitment to working with colleagues<br><br><br><br>—Internal quality of teaching as a profession<br>—Social negotiation; Crisis |
| **Coding Memo:**<br>Culture, values, and attitudes are factors for considering primary school physical education teachers' (PSPETs) work Lives. Check and be sensitive if informants make similar comments or have similar experiences. These might lead to an exploration of their professionalization process. ||

**Figure 7.6:** Example of Interview Transcript and Open Coding From: https://www.researchgate.net/publication/260126435_Diversified_professionalism_of_physical_education_teachers_in_the_Asian_context_of_Hong_Kong/figures?lo=1

> **Question** In your peer-review group, examine Figure 7.6 or 7.7 and determine what might be the topic/research question(s) of the study that would generate the illustrated answer from a participant? Additionally, looking at the raw data and preliminary codes, what one or two other final codes could you derive from the interview segment?

# Chapter 7: Data Fluency: The Foundations of Quantitative and Qualitative Data Analysis

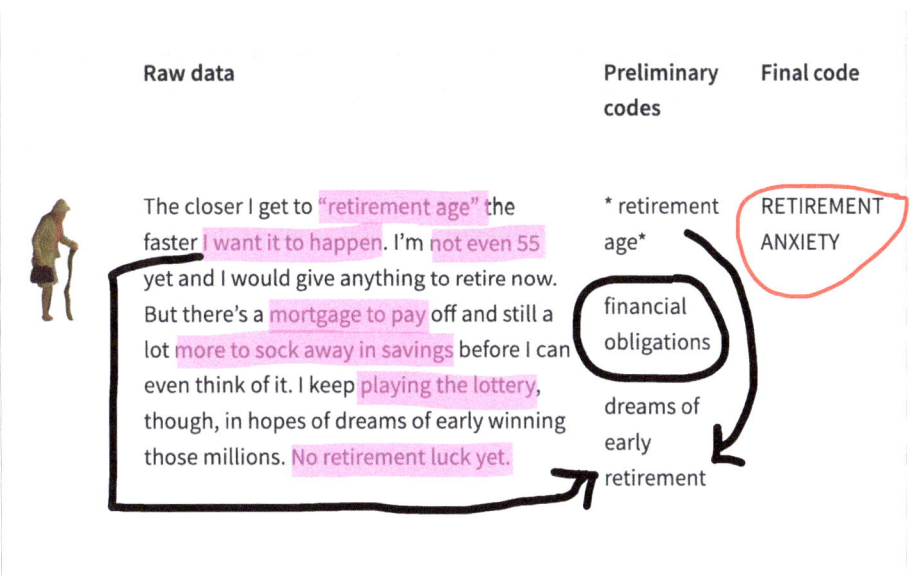

**Figure 7.7:** Coding Example
Adapted from: https://www.cessda.eu/Training/Training-Resources/Library/Data-Management-Expert-Guide/3.-Process/Qualitative-coding

## 7.4 | Application

*Finding themes and patterns in data: What do data tell us?*

"Research is to see what everybody has seen and think what nobody has thought."

Albert Szent-Gyorgyi

> **Food for Thought** Reflect on the quote at the start of this section. In what way(s) are the practitioners well placed in their professional environments to formulate research questions/inquiries/topics for investigation, and how this positionality might impact analysis?

Now that you collected both quantitative and qualitative data, it is essential to talk *about* these data and *talk through* these data. These aloud discussions are a good practice to adopt for the initial stages of any analysis. If you think about this practice for a bit, that is how we (in the human world) often make sense of things.

Time and lapses of time are also necessary. A bit of time has passed since you worked with quantitative data (Chapter 4), and although you recently completed qualitative data collection, some time has passed since you thought about your qualitative protocols. This is good—these time-lapses and breaks to do "other things" between thinking about data, data collection, data synopsis, and analysis is actually a very good thing—you need this time to separate from your research and then revisit. The process of separation provides clarity for new ideas and the ability to see what nobody has thought. For these and the following reasons, we will be brief here. Much of what we were hoping you could apply in this chapter as you continue to add to your skillset of using research as a *tool* belongs in a workshop setting through multiple interactions with your peers and professor.

If possible, for this application section, we would like you to provide and receive support from your peer-review partner or peer-review group that you joined back in the day when you were reading Chapter 3. Peer review and collaboration is how many, if not all, professional researchers keep each other honest and provide feedback based on shared expertise—we suggest you adopt a similar practice, if not always, at least for this segment and assignment below. The primary purpose of this collaboration would be to ensure that significant elements in the analysis and interpretation of raw data are not missed. As a point of clarification, all peer work must be done in parallel, and as a support mechanism for one another, peer review and support does NOT mean a group project; you must be the sole author of your work.

Revisit quantitative data: With your newly acquired knowledge of data analysis from this chapter, revisit the assignment completed in Chapter 4 and take a closer look at what the data are depicting through the following lens: *How the quantitative data you collected illustrate an equity disparity(ies) at your selected school site?* As you reengage with these data, keep the context of the school site in mind (as your main point of focus) and as relevant to your topic/research question(s). Then assess how the district and the state's data as a whole relate (or not) to the school site. Next, take turns explaining the trends to your peer-review partner(s). As you describe, flush out some of the patterns you observe in the data and discuss possible similarities/differences between what you and your peers are finding. This process will help you understand/analyze data better and *"talk through"* the evidence. During this discussion or at the end, document your additional findings by adding to your synopsis of data; while doing so, consider the following: Are your analysis of these quantitative data (i.e., school site, district, state) similar or different in light of your topic/research questions? In what ways and how? Use the quantitative trends in the descriptive data to expand on your earlier interpretation of findings. Your synopsis of quantitative data is foundational for future analysis and as the next step of engagement with the qualitative data.

Now that you have collected and transcribed the three sources of data (or if you are engaging in content analysis, obtained a primary school site document), it is time to review and discuss the raw qualitative data with your peer-review partner(s) to start thinking about potential codes and themes that might be emerging. As you discuss possible codes with your colleagues, rely on the information presented and examples provided in Section 7.3 of this chapter. Next, take turns with your peers to read aloud and talk through the emergent codes. These discussions with peers who share similar interests are the beginning of analysis and will help navigate the next data interpretation steps as outlined in the assignment section of this chapter (Section 7.7).

## 7.5 | Conclusion

In this chapter, we provided an overview of foundations in data analysis techniques concerning quantitative and qualitative research. Practitioners, scholars, and educators spend entire careers developing appropriate data analysis techniques for specific data types and methodologies. As you are experiencing throughout this course, every topic, population of interest, data collection approach, selected methodology, analysis techniques, and ensuing conclusions hold particular considerations, exceptions, caveats, and competing frameworks. However, your ability to grasp these themes and concepts at a fundamental level will allow you to receive, examine, and interpret data in an educated and defined manner.

## 7.6 | Discussion

1. As an educator and/or aspiring administrator, why do you think it is important to describe the population sample that was included in a study?
2. School site or central demographic student data help you understand the students you are either working with or will be serving. Think about and list three to five quantitative measures that you could gather and summarize to understand your student population In addition to the quantitative

# Chapter 7: Data Fluency: The Foundations of Quantitative and Qualitative Data Analysis

data, please tell us what additional qualitative information would add value to understanding your student profile. Please answer this question while relying on school/district examples and data synthesis.

3. Think about what you had learned from Sections 7.2 and 7.3, why do you think researchers place such an emphasis on transparency and replicability?
4. Circle back to the subsection on coding (see Section 7.3), why do you think it is critical to keep detailed annotations during a research study? And how do these could potentially impact the analysis of qualitative data?
5. "Reducing the predictive power of demographics" is a term used to say "our goal is to close the achievement gap." What are the demographics that are being referenced when we make this statement? Can you cite measures (qualitative or quantitative) where there are no gaps?
6. Different environmental issues during different academic years can cause the need for learning acceleration. Describe and summarize the data that you are using in your current careers (e.g., classroom, at school site) to determine how many students are in need of learning acceleration?
7. After the COVID-19 pandemic, the return to in-person instruction has undoubtedly been a strain on educators and educational leaders with countless benefits for students. What are two to three themes that you would describe have emerged with supporting quotes from different stakeholder groups (e.g., students, school staff, and families) to summarize the return to in-person instruction?
8. What are the data needed (quantitative and qualitative) to construct school site plans? Compile a list. Looking at this list of data, describe the statistics to be used to summarize the findings. Of all measures cited, which data and summary are most essential to the school site plan?

## 7.7 | Assignment: Qualitative and Quantitative Data as the Building Blocks of Analysis

Now that you have a better understanding of quantitative and qualitative data analysis, and engaged in application of newly learned knowledge (preferably with the help from your peers) the next step is to expand upon the quantitative assignment (Section 4.7) and engage in analysis of your recently collected qualitative data (Chapter 6) by creating a systematic record of codes and deriving final themes to further inform quantitative findings through equity gap analysis of all data sources.

**STEP 1: Quantitative data reexamination** *(use Working Data Analysis Template)*: Cut and paste the three tables and quantitative data synopsis write-up (Section 4.7: Assignment: Quantitative Exercise and Synthesis) as well as any additional interpretation of data you added as you engaged with the application section of this chapter (Section 7.4). Continue to reexamine these longitudinal data from an existing equity disparity. Ask yourself a few questions and start drafting the analysis of these data (*be brief but on-point, no more than one ten-sentence paragraph*) with the following questions in mind:

- How are trends performing over time for each level of data? In general, are percentages changing over time?
- Looking across the three levels of data, are any of the levels performing better than the others?
- How does this data inform your research topic of interest?
- What is missing from this data that you wish you could answer?

**STEP 2: Qualitative data interpretation, coding, and salient themes** *(use Working Data Analysis Template)*: Now it is time to take a look at the qualitative data. First, briefly describe your qualitative data for the record (see Table 7.4 in Working Data Analysis Template). Then examine the structure outlined in Table 7.5 of the Working Data Analysis Template and cut/paste your raw data into the designated column for each data source. After engaging your qualitative data, what are some of the codes that are emerging? Use a highlighter function in Word to highlight codes (use different colors for different codes) and provide either open coding interpretation (see Figure 7.6 in Section 7.3) or list preliminary and then final codes as shown in Figure 7.7 (Section 7.3). *Remember, your qualitative data is designed to deepen your understanding of the quantitative findings*—keep this in mind as you code. After, determine the final themes as evidenced in the data and draft your synthesis and analysis of data substantiated by direct (but brief) quotes from interviews, discussions, documents, and so on, to support your findings. As with the quantitative analysis, your write-up should be concise; however, expect it to be more extensive since you will need to include direct quotes.

**STEP 3: Joint analysis of the equity issue** *(use Working Data Analysis Template):* Now that you finished analyzing two sources of data, you can clearly identify the equity issue. Use the quantitative analysis as primary and qualitative analysis as secondary (to further inform your quantitative results) combine the two analyses sections. While doing so, draw from sources included in your annotated bibliography as well as synthesis of the literature (Chapter 5) to further substantiate your analysis. Speak to (with evidence) *how the qualitative data sources have helped you strengthen your understanding of the quantitative data? Based on the themes derived from the qualitative segment of data collection and interpretation, what are the possible explanations for the persistent equity gap as identified in interviews from staff, parents, administrators, and/or your observations, and/or through an examination of school documents? In what way/ways do your analysis of these data are alike or different from what is reported in the literature?*

## WORKING DATA ANALYSIS TEMPLATE

**Indicator:**

**Topic:**

**Research question(s):**

**Research methodology:**

### Synthesis of Scholarly Literature

[Cut/paste from Section 5.9: Qualitative Synthesis (ONLY include the synthesis—brief literature review—of the assignment)]

### Quantitative Data

[see STEP 1: Quantitative data reexamination]

### Quantitative Data Record

*(Cut/paste from Section 4.7: Assignment: Quantitative Exercise and Synthesis)*

Table 7.1: School Site *(3 years of data with population of focus highlighted)*

Table 7.2: District *(3 years of data with population of focus highlighted)*

Table 7.3: The State *(3 years of data with population of focus highlighted)*

### Quantitative Data Analysis

[*Be brief but on-point, no more than one five/ten-sentence paragraph*]

## Qualitative Data

[See STEP 2: Qualitative data interpretation, coding, and salient themes]

### Qualitative Data Record

**Table 7.4:** Qualitative Sources, Method of Analysis and Description: [include topic and population of focus here]

| # | Data Source | Data Collection Method | Description |
|---|---|---|---|
| 1 | e.g., Math teachers of students are English Language Learners (ELL) | e.g., interview | e.g., Conducted interview to discuss the equity gap in mathematics between ELLs and English-only students |
| 2 | e.g., Students | e.g., focus group discussion/ interview | e.g., Unstructured focus group discussion with ELLs to understand their challenges in learning math in a traditional classroom setting |
| 3 | e.g., content delivery | e.g., observation | e.g., Own unstructured observations of math content delivery in a traditional classroom setting |

**Table 7.5:** Working Table of Raw Qualitative Data, Data Coding, and Final Themes

| # | RAW Data Transcript | Coding/open coding | Final code/ theme |
|---|---|---|---|
| 1 | INTERVIEW: MATH TEACHER<br>Q:<br>A:<br>Q:<br>A: | | |
| 2 | FOCUS GROUP DISCUSSION/INTERVIEW: STUDENTS<br>Q:<br>A:<br>Q:<br>A: | | |

| 3 | CLASSROOM OBSERVATION NOTES<br>Setting:<br>Dynamics:<br>Conversations:<br>*(Add fields as appropriate or organized in your notes per protocol)* | | |
|---|---|---|---|

**Qualitative Data Synthesis and Analysis**

[*Be brief but on-point and include direct quotes to substantiate your themes/findings*]

Theme 1

Theme 2

Theme 3

### Equity Gap Analysis

[See STEP 3: Joint data analysis of the equity issue]

# References

Austin, G., Hanson, T., Polik, J., & Zheng, C. (2018). *School climate, substance use, and well-being among California students 2015–2017: Results of the sixteenth biennial statewide student survey,* Grades 7, 9, and 11. WestEd. https://data.calschls.org/resources/Biennial_State_1517.pdf

Corbin, J. M., & Anselm, S. (1990). Grounded theory research: Procedures, canons, and evaluative criteria. *Qualitative Sociology, 13(1),* 3–12. https://doi.org/10.1007/BF00988593

ESRI. (2014). *Oakland unified school district uses GIS to further academic achievement.* ARCNEWS. https://www.esri.com/about/newsroom/arcnews/oakland-unified-school-district-uses-gis-to-further-academic-achievement/?rmedium=arcnews&rsource=https://www.esri.com/esri-news/arcnews/winter1314articles/oakland-unified-school-district-uses-gis-to-further-aca

Gibbs, G.R. (2007). *Thematic Coding and Categorizing, Analyzing Qualitative Data.* SAGE Publications Ltd., London. http://dx.doi.org/10.4135/9781849208574

Khandkar, S. H. (n.d.). *Open Coding.* Retrieved from: http://pages.cpsc.ucalgary.ca/~saul/wiki/uploads/CPSC681/open-coding.pdf

Lester, J. N., Cho, Y., & Lochmiller, C. R. (2020). Learning to do qualitative data analysis: A starting point. *Human Resource Development Review, 19(1),* 94–106. https://doi.org/10.1177/1534484320903890

Thorne, S. (2000). Data analysis in qualitative research. *Evidence Based Nursing, 3(3),* 68–70. https://doi.org/10.1136/ebn.3.3.68

Yin, R. K. (2013). Validity and generalization in future case study evaluations. *Evaluation, 19(3),* 321–332. https://doi.org/10.1177/1356389013497081

# CHAPTER 8

# Formulating a Problem Statement: Key Elements in Academic Writing and Research Direction

*Now what? Data collected, analysis completed, what's next?*

## 8.1 | Introduction

In this chapter, we unpack the basics of the writing style used in the field of education. You do not need to be an expert in the style, but you need to understand the basics and know where to look when stuck. We include the most common issues that our students typically ask us about, for example, how to reference in text, what goes into a list of references, among few other items, so that this text will serve not only as a textbook but also as a reference guide. Of course, you are welcome to purchase the manual if you like, but with then information available online and the basics included in this text, we are sure you will get by!

Going over the basics of the writing style is necessary as you move through the next steps and assignments requiring more writing. This chapter discusses the next phase of your thus far engagements that lead to formulating and writing a problem statement. We conclude with an application, discussion, and assignment sections. All of which are designed to make you think through the problem (the equity gap in your equity gap analysis), organize your thoughts, and finally compose a problem statement to be used as a basis for creating a plan for improvement or a research proposal.

## 8.2 | The Nitty-gritty of Writing in Education: The American Psychological Association and all *That* Mess

We are well aware that you have been doing much writing in this course, as well as other courses in your graduate/post baccalaureate program, not to mention you were writing as an undergraduate student, of course! Writing is a significant part of an academic life. And, although we might have dreaded writing back in the day or still dread certain type of writing, the technological advances did not ease the burden of writing, but rather amplified the need for writing and communicating through writing. Daily texts messages, emails, social media accounts, just to name a few, all require writing—albeit not all are of academic nature, but nonetheless. Put simply, writing is an important part of our lives and our field is no exception. After all, we do much writing in education so it is important to review the basic principles of the writing style we adhere to.

While many of you used Modern Language Association (MLA) style in your English classes, Chicago style in your history courses, American Sociological Association (ASA) when you took sociology, among many others, Education subscribes to **American Psychological Association (APA) style**. That is the style of our field and it is expected that when we write reports, complete assignments, compose presentations, we adhere to APA.

This said, you do not need to know EVERYTHING about APA to adhere to the style in your writing, but having a solid foundational awareness about this style is an important tool to master, especially if you are one of the candidates vying for a position within educational administration. When stuck, of course, you can always consult the plethora of information available on the internet or purchase the latest APA style guide to be included on your desk as one of your "go to" texts. What we would like to cover in this section are a few useful items about the APA style to help you as you write and assist with looking APA up when stuck.

## APA Issue Number One: Stylistic

Aside from the technical aspects of APA several of which we cover below, there are a number of stylistic items that you need to keep in mind when writing in APA style (also see Table 8.1). APA publication manual calls on the authors to write clearly and concisely. As you tighten-up your writing, there are two important items: **(1) APA style writing is formal** and should adopt to a tone that is appropriate for the professional context/communication with the colleagues in professional settings. That is, with other researchers or practitioners. Therefore, avoid abbreviation (don't, can't, won't etc.—write these out), the use of slang, or other nonformal elements. **(2) APA style is straightforward where ideas are communicated simply and clearly**. When writing in APA style, the focus should always be on the ideas themselves and not on how these are communicated. To achieve this: keep your sentences clear, short, and direct; when relaying on what other authors/research in the field reported about a topic (e.g., when writing a literature review or when substantiating your own findings/claims), avoid the use of direct quotes and paraphrase as much as possible—APA discourages overuse of direct quotes since it takes away from the clarity of writing—use direct quotes *only* when you cannot say it better than the author, for example, in cases of providing a definition for a term that has been coined, or relaying a phrase that carries a particular insight about a topic; technical terms must be used to improve communication and add clarity and should *not* take away from clarity of writing; and, avoid bias when writing for the sake of objectivity and accuracy (see Table 8.2).

**Table 8.1:** Features of APA Style Writing

Adapted from: https://opentextbc.ca/researchmethods/chapter/american-psychological-association-apa-style/#return-footnote-958-3

| APA style feature | Scientific value or assumption |
| --- | --- |
| There are very few direct quotations of other researchers. | The phenomena and theories of psychology are objective and do not depend on the specific words a particular researcher used to describe them. |
| Criticisms are directed at other researchers' work but not at them personally. | The focus of scientific research is on drawing general conclusions about the world, not on the personalities of particular researchers. |
| There are many references and reference citations. | Scientific research is a large-scale collaboration among many researchers. |
| Empirical research reports are organized with specific sections in a fixed order. | There is an ideal approach to conducting empirical research in psychology (even if this ideal is not always achieved in actual research). |
| Researchers tend to "hedge" their conclusions, e.g., "The results *suggest* that . . ." | Scientific knowledge is tentative and always subject to revision based on new empirical results. |

# Chapter 8: Formulating a Problem Statement

**Table 8.2:** Examples of Avoiding Bias When Writing in APA

| Instead of . . . | Use . . . |
|---|---|
| Special education students/students with disabilities | Students with special needs |
| Hispanic | Latino/a or LatinX |
| Minority students | Students of color |
| Men | Men and women, people |
| Limited English proficient students | English learner students or emergent bilingual students |

## APA Issue Number Two: Basic In-text Application of APA

Know the basic technical application of APA, such as how to cite in-text, how to cite direct quotes (including those that are lengthy – yes, lengthy quotes are cited differently!), the rules for using acronyms, and how to present numerical writing. These are the very basics that go a long way and solve many APA problems if learned/mastered (see Table 8.3 for common issues and examples).

**Table 8.3:** Common In-text APA Issues and Examples

| Common APA issues | Examples |
|---|---|
| **Citing in-text narrative citation** when *paraphrasing* | Although many people believe that women are more talkative than men, Mehl, Vazire, Ramirez-Esparza, Slatcher, and Pennebaker (2007) found essentially no difference in the number of words spoken by male and female college students. |
| **Citing in-text parenthetical citation** *when paraphrasing* | Recent evidence suggests that men and women are similarly talkative (Mehl, Vazire, Ramirez-Esparza, Slatcher, & Pennebaker, 2007).<br><br>[*notice the period is placed after in-text citation*] |
| **Citing in-text parenthetical citation** multiple authors *when paraphrasing* | Recent evidence suggests that men and women are similarly talkative (Mehl, Vazire, Ramirez-Esparza, Slatcher, & Pennebaker, 2007; Vegas, 2011; Wong 2009).<br><br>[*notice the alphabetical, NOT chronological order. Also, once you list all authors in a multi-author citation once, you can just include "et al." thereafter, e.g., (Mehle et al., 2007)*] |
| **Direct quotes (short)**—all direct quotes MUST include a page number | It was noted in the study that "students often had difficulty using APA style" (Jones, 1998, p. 199), but the author did offer a detailed explanation for the reported difficulties with APA style. |
| **Direct quotes (long)**—if more than three lines, the entire quote should be indented by half an inch |     Students had difficulty using APA style, especially when it was their first-time citing sources. This difficulty could have been attributed to the fact that many students failed to purchase APA style manual and did not have other reliable references to know how to cite per APA.<br><br>                                                      (Jones, 1998, p. 199)<br><br>[*notice no quotation marks when indented*] |
| **Acronyms** must be written out when used in text for the first time—after that you can just use the acronym | While many of you used Modern Language Association (MLA) style in your English classes, Chicago style in your history courses, American Sociological Association (ASA) style when you took sociology, the field of Education subscribes to American Psychological Association (APA) style. |

| Common APA issues | Examples |
|---|---|
| **Numbers up to ten** must be written out. | Due to shortages, we were only able to obtain seven APA style guides for a class of 18 graduate students. |
| **Numbers that appearing at the start of sentence** must be written out. | Thirty nine percent of the students were able to access APA style guide. |

Common In-text APA Issues & Examples. Cite as: Okhremtchouk, Irina S., et. al.; Price, Paul C., et. al.; and Purdue Online Writing Lab.

## APA Issue Number Three: Organization

Lastly, know the basics of organization as outlined by APA. That is, how to organize your APA paper (e.g., cover page, etc.), introduce a running had, the use of different level headings, and how to organize a list of references—please note that the list of references is called something else in different styles, so if you use anything else than "Reference" at the end of your paper, it is an easy give-away that you might be straggling with APA format.

**Table 8.4:** APA (Seventh Edition) Organization and Examples

| What | Example |
|---|---|
| **Headings** | **Heading Level 1**<br>[Used for major sections: center, bold, capitalized]<br>Text on the new line<br><br>**Heading Level 2**<br>[A section within a major section: left aligned, bold, capitalized]<br>Text on the new line<br><br>*Heading Level 3*<br>[A subsection for Level 2: left aligned, bold, italicized and capitalized]<br>Text on the new line<br><br>    **Heading Level 4.** Text on the same line<br>    [A subsection for Level 3: indented, bold, and capitalized]<br><br>    *Heading Level 5.* Text on the same line<br>    [A subsection for Level 4: indented, bold, italicized, and capitalized] |
| **Running head and page numbers** | RUNNING HEAD ALL CAPITAL LETTERS    1<br>[All CAP letters and no more than 50 characters. Page numbers are included in the top right corner, excluding cover page. Use Word functions: Header and Footer View and Page Numbers under Insert] |
| **Empirical research reports** have several distinct sections that always appear in the same order | **Title page.** Presents the article title and author names and affiliations.<br>**Abstract page.** Summarizes the research.<br>**Introduction.** Introduces the study and provides rationale for the current study.<br>**Literature Review.** Describes previous research and how this extant work is relevant for the current study.<br>**Method.** Describes how the study was conducted.<br>**Results.** Describes the results of the study.<br>**Discussion.** Summarizes the study and discusses its implications.<br>**References.** Lists the references cited throughout the article. |

| What | Example |
|---|---|
| References page: Notice the citations for different sources | **References**<br>Author's last name, Initial(s). (Year of publication). *Title of the book*. Publisher. https://doi.org/DOI<br>Author's last name, Initial(s). (Year of publication). Title of the article. *Title of Journal, Volume*(Issue), Pages. https://doi.org/DOI<br>Author's last name, Initial(s). (Year, Month Day of publication). *Title of the work*. Website. https://URL<br>Author's last name, Initial(s). (Year of publication). Title of the article. *Newspaper*. https://URL<br>Last name, Initial(s). [Channel]. (Year, Month Day of publication). *Title of the video* [Video]. Website. https://URL<br>Organization. (Year of publication). Word. In *Dictionary*. Publisher. https://URL |

As you are regularly using the APA style, we hope that this section proved helpful and serves as a quick reference. The bottom line is that the uniformity and consistency of adhering to a style help readers focus on the ideas being presented and gives readers an option to scan texts for key points, findings, and resources. Therefore, when we write, we must think about our readers first and foremost—this reminder is necessary for the next section of this chapter as we discuss the problem statement and its applicability. We also included a list of online APA sources and provided templates in the supplemental resources section of this text.

## 8.3 | Conveying a Problem in a Problem Statement

Now that we got the basics of APA style out of the way, it is time to discuss the problem statement. We are confident that you either wrote, attempted to write, or at the very least heard about problem statements, but could you define what a problem statement is? Or, better yet, could you write one based on the examination of your topic? What is a problem statement? And what goes into it? Many would agree with us that in order to produce a decent quality product, one needs to know what it is and what goes into it. Thus, whether you are a pro in the subject of problem statements, need a refresher, or need to learn more about it, let us unpack it together.

### A Problem Statement: Definition

A problem statement is a direct and concrete outline of an issue to be addressed or a problem to be improved. A problem statement must be clear, unambiguous and substantiated by evidence. It is written with a specific audience in mind to communicate the issue or a problem, as well as its urgency. It outlines the gaps between how things are now (currently) and the desired direction. It must be grounded in data (be evidence-based) and outline facts (including those specific to the context). A problem statement should also include a call to action that is audience-specific and, preferably, inspirational to obtain a buy-in from others. The five Ws and a HOW provide a structure for a problem statement. That is, consider the following when writing a problem statement: *who, what, when, where, why, and how*? Do remember that your problem statement should be concise, we suggest keeping it to 500 words (one double-spaced page) and no more than 750 words (a page and a half double-spaced).

### The Purpose of a Problem Statement is to . . .
1. **Introduce the reader to the importance of the topic being studied**. The reader is oriented to the significance of the problem or study.

2. **Anchor the research questions, hypotheses, or assumptions to follow**. It offers a concise statement about the purpose.
3. **Place the topic into a particular context** that defines the parameters of what is to be done (in practice) or investigated (in research).
4. **Provide the framework for reporting the results** and indicates what is likely necessary to make improvements or conduct the study and explain how the findings will present this information.

## A Problem Statement: In Research

Likewise, a research problem statement is not much different form the general definition. It must include a direct, clear, and unambiguous definition about an area of concern or an existing gap in extant literature, or theory, or within practice. The difference in the case of a research problem statement is that it must call for a meaningful understanding of the issue and deliberate investigation. This said, the "so what?" question is frequently posed in the case of research problem statements. The Research Guide from the University of Southern California outlines how to survive the "so what?" question—we include their advice below.

## To Survive the "So What" Question, Problem Statements Should Possess the Following Attributes

- Clarity and precision [A well-written statement does not make sweeping generalizations and irresponsible pronouncements; it also does include unspecific determinates like "very" or "giant"]
- Demonstrate a researchable topic or issue [i.e., feasibility of conducting the study is based upon access to information that can be effectively acquired, gathered, interpreted, synthesized, and understood]
- Identification of what would be studied, while avoiding the use of value-laden words and terms
- Identification of an overarching question or small set of questions accompanied by key factors or variables
- Identification of key concepts and terms
- Articulation of the study's conceptual boundaries or parameters or limitations
- Some generalizability in regards to applicability and bringing results into general use
- Conveyance of the study's importance, benefits, and justification [i.e., regardless of the type of research, it is important to demonstrate that the research is not trivial]
- Does not have unnecessary jargon or overly complex sentence constructions
- Conveyance of more than the mere gathering of descriptive data providing only a snapshot of the issue or phenomenon under investigation

## The Problem in a Problem Statement

Whether your problem statement addresses an issue or a gap found in practice or research, you must have a problem to work with! As you identify a problem, the problem you identify must be grounded in evidence. In a nutshell, without grounding your problem in evidence, you do not have a problem! We ask that you remember this when drafting your problem statement as part of the application and assignment sections later in this chapter.

So now, let us talk about evidence. Through prior discussions and engagements in this textbook, you have learned that evidence is derived from data. That is, evidence can be generated by prior research that examined and/or analyzed data (e.g., scholarly literature, see your annotated bibliography from Chapter 3) and/or through one's own topic/research question and investigation (e.g., your thus far engagements including quantitative synthesis, qualitative data collection, and data analysis), or better yet, both! As you have noticed from reading scholarly literature, it is both. Likewise, we guided you through the process of using research as a tool in this text, we also laid out all the steps involved in a sequential examination effectively leading to establishing concrete evidence about an issue or a problem of practice, which you outlined in the equity gap analysis (Chapter 7). We did this intentionally, so you could not only read about research/evidence presented by others but also employ research as a tool to establish evidence for your topic of interest.

Let us review:

- Your problem must be backed by evidence or you have no problem!
  - Evidence could be (a) prior research where data helped formulate evidence
  - Evidence could be (b) your own investigation by means of examining data
  - The best way to establish evidence is to employ both! That is have an understanding of prior research/scholarly works/research-backed best practices AND gather your own data, effectively creating a stronger argument for the identified problem

> **Question** Discuss "The Problem in a Problem Statement" section with your peer-review partner or in a small group. Then think of situations when employing both evidence from literature and gathering your own data might not be possible. Once you identify such situations, what might be an effective way to circumvent these and still generate a strong problem statement that is evidence based?

## 8.4 | Basic Elements of Next Steps After the Problem Statement

### Plan for Improvement and Research Proposal

There is more than one way to address the problem you identified in a problem statement. The problems identified in practice would necessitate a plan for improvement or a plan of engaging in Action Research (more on action research in Chapter 9) where one engages in improving own professional practice or learning more about the problem while in action, that is, Action Research. Or, constructing a plan to further investigate the issue identified in a research problem statement, that is, a research proposal. We unpack important essentials to consider as you select to engage in either one or the other.

### Plan for Improvement: Education Leadership

Assuming that your area of interest is of practical nature/to improve practice and education leadership is your long- or short-term goal, consider designing a plan for improvement. That is, once you construct a problem statement (more on problem statement in application and assignment sections), developing a data-driven/evidence-based improvement plan is the next step. And although we do not go into details of the improvement plan here (a different class!), we do outline several features that such a plan would require to be successful.

Perhaps one of the essential features is robust contextual knowledge. Contextual knowledge is necessary to ensure contextual applicability. A close second is buy-in from stakeholders. Without addressing these two items, one would run into problems when implementing a plan, no matter how well it is structured or grounded in evidence. It is also important to consider that what might be contextually appropriate for one school site would be unacceptable for another. And, if key stakeholders are not on board for implementing the plan, then there goes the entire plan. Thus, context plus buy-in amount to success and must be considered when designing such a plan.

If a plan for improvement is your next step, then take time to think through and design strategies for implementation that are context-appropriate. Remember, these strategies need to be evidence-based; in this case/while designing strategies, you will be relying on best practices as identified in the scholarly literature for evidence. Also, remember to include the overarching goal and objective for each strategy and expected short- and long-term desired outcomes. Limit your strategies to anywhere between three and five total; any more than five would be overwhelming. Again, don't forget to contextualize these, that is, how would these particular strategies work in the school/context you are proposing? After you draft your plan for improvement, the next step would be to have it reviewed by the stakeholders. It is permissible to use experts outside of the school site context as one layer of review (in fact, at times, it might be beneficial to gain an outside perspective); however, the majority of the reviewers you choose should come from the context (i.e., the school site) for which you are designing your plan since the buy-in or the lack thereof will make or break your proposed plan. With this in mind and before approaching stakeholders to review your plant, you want to consider the following two questions: (1) Who will be on the frontlines executing the plan? and (2) Who will be on the receiving end of the plan? Once you identify these individuals, you want to acquire their feedback since, although not guaranteed, this will bring your plan closer to establishing buy-in with the stakeholders.

> **Exercise** With your peer-review partner(s), circle back to your topic, data, and equity gap analysis. Then brainstorm what strategies might go into your plan for improvement and discuss how these strategies align with the context of your school sites. Then make a shortlist of key stakeholders from whom you plan to obtain feedback. Finally, take turns talking through the strategies and stakeholder lists aloud while explaining your selections. As you discuss, remember to both receive and offer feedback.

## Research Proposal: A Path to a Larger Study

If your future aspirations include a larger study based on or similar to the topic/equity gap issue you identified as part of your thus far investigation, then your problem statement needs to align with the elements of a research problem statement (see Section 8.3). Now, your interests may include both, that is, designing a plan for improvement and research proposal, which is great! However, for the purposes of this chapter and to keep your focus aligned, we ask that you select one or the other.

More on the research proposals. Once you formulate a research problem statement, the next step is to write a research proposal. A research proposal is a proposal outlining a need for a future study and method for investigation. It follows a uniformly accepted outline that includes the following sections that encapsulate a plant for forthcoming research:

- Proposed title of your future study
    - Research topic (i.e., explain the problem and *what* you plan to research)
        - Research question(s) encompassing your topic and population of focus
    - Your justification for the proposed study backed by evidence (i.e., a literature review outlining extant literature and *why* the proposed topic is worth researching—i.e., what gaps does the proposed project aims to fill based on the extant literature?)
    - The method and steps for data collection and analysis (i.e., outline a methodology to be used as a template for *how* you plan to investigate
        - That is, what are your participants; how you plan to engage in data collection; how do you plan to analyze these data analysis?)
    - A timeframe for the proposed study

The purpose of a research proposal is to persuade your academic advisor and/or select academic committee and/or a group of colleagues that your research is appropriate as it relates to your area of study/need AND that it is doable within the proposed timeframe. As we guided you through engagements within this text, you naturally progressed through the steps necessary in a research proposal. We suggest leaning on your problem statement to engage in an act of persuasion, since convincing your advisor/committee/colleagues will be the key element in moving forward with your investigation. The resource section of this book includes an outline of a research proposal template.

> **Exercise** With your peer-review partner(s), circle back to your topic/research questions, data, and equity gap analysis. Then brainstorm what a larger or next research project might look like considering either a similar topic/population of focus or taking your gained knowledge and thinking about the next direction of research/research topic. Additionally, think about the appropriate method to employ in your investigation based on the topic for future research. Finally, take turns with your peers talking about your research topics and methods you are thinking about using. As you discuss, remember to both receive and offer feedback.

## 8.5 | Application: Writing a Problem Statement *Data Collected, Analysis Completed, What's Next?*

*What is next?* Now that you learned more about academic writing in the field of education (APA format and style), what a problem statement should include compositionally, the two types of problem statements (practice and research-oriented), it is time to discuss the organization side of the problem statements and start organizing. Similar to the application section in the previous chapter (Chapter 7), it would be best for you to connect with your peer-review partner(s) as we unpack the organizational side of things in this application section and as you prepare for your upcoming assignment.

First, decide on the direction of your problem statement—talk it over with your peers and professor. Then, ask yourself the following question: *What direction do I want to take as my next step, e.g., practical application or research proposal?* We realize that you might be thinking about both—if so, we reached our goal of making you think about research as a tool! But for this application engagement, we would like you to select one or the other. Once you make your selection, move to the second item below.

Second, start organizing! Since your problem statement is school site-specific, make sure to know what the school's vision and mission are and have these available at your fingertips. Many if not all schools post this information on their website, look this information up, and have it in front of you. In rare cases, you might not be able to find the school site's vision and mission statements. In that case, use the one established by the school district.[1] We ask you to look into the school site's mission and vision because, as you contextualize and ground your problem statement, it is essential to use the school site's vision and mission statements to ground your statement, hence establishing the context. Additionally, you will need your annotated bibliography as a quick reference to help you substantiate your claims with in-text citations. You will also need the synopsis of literature you wrote as part of the Chapter 5 assignment to help you with the framing. Make sure to have quantitative and qualitative data and analysis close by to talk about and cite concrete data from your investigation. Last but not least, you will need your equity gap analysis. Your equity gap analysis narrative is critical in framing the problem statement since it brings all the data (quantitative and qualitative) and evidence together by situating the problem in the context of your school. Once you gather the above-listed items, you will be ready for the third item.

Third, after gathering all the items, talk through everything you have with your peers and visualize how your problem statement might look like. Circle back to Section 8.3 of this chapter to remind yourselves about the composition structure of a problem statement, be it practice or research-oriented.

---

[1] Only use the district's visions and mission statements if your selected school site does not have these. As you develop your problem statement, make sure to explain why you used the district's mission and vision statements and not that of the school's since the school is your entity of focus.

Ask: *In what way do I need to frame my problem statement to make it convincing to the staff at the school and possibly leadership at the district? How do I create a buy-in? Think of ways of presenting the evidence to ground your statement. Think about why should staff follow you/your direction as you unpack the problem to be addressed in practice? Or recognize the need for a more extensive research study?*

Think of ways to tie your problem statement to the site's vision and mission statements. As you brainstorm, do not brainstorm alone—share and discuss your thoughts and reservations with your peer-review partner(s). Take turns sharing and offering feedback while taking notes on what is discussed, so nothing is missed.

Fourth, create an outline in preparation for your upcoming assignment. Remember, a concise, clear, and well-conveyed problem statement is paramount to finding and implementing effective solutions. Your problem statement should be a stand-alone document anywhere between 500 and 750 words. Depending on the direction of your problem statement (practical or research), it might convey different urgency for the next steps. This said, however, all problem statements follow a similar organizational process. Here is an outline as you begin to organize:

**Title**

**Name and contextualize the problem** (the equity gap that you identified through your investigation and data analysis) by including data/evidence and substantiating these by citing academic literature—make sure to tie the problem/equity gap to the school's mission and vision to ground the equity gap in context

**Show why the problem matters** by discussing why is it important that the problem is either addressed in practice OR researched further to find solutions?

**Practical application:**
*What will happen if the problem is not solved?*
*Who will feel the consequences?*
*Does the problem have wider relevance, a potential snowball effect?*
**Research application:**
*What are the gaps in extant literature?*
*Why further research is needed on the topic?*
*How will resolving the problem or expanding our understanding of the topic will help us resolve the problem?*
*What benefits will it have for future research and practice?*

**Provide direction**—The goal here is not to outline a conclusive solution, but discuss possible reasons (Hint: rely on your qualitative data analysis/themes) behind the problem and discuss direction for more effective approaches to either tackle the problem (practical application) or deepen understanding (research application). *What should be the goal(s) and objective(s)?*

## 8.6 | Conclusion

Writing well and writing in style is foundational to establishing effective communication no matter your role within the field of Education. Identifying and conveying a problem is critical, especially in the field of educational leadership. It is impossible to create organizational change or inspire colleagues and staff to take a leap in changing their practices or approaches without a strong ability to formulate and convey a problem. As you progress in your career within the field of education, we genuinely hope that you continue to use this text as a guide and reference to address the equity gap issues and make change possible.

## 8.7 | Discussion

1. What are some of the resources that you could reference/cite when (a) writing your papers (in your courses) and (b) while compiling reports at your current job? Please delineate these resource(s) and their use.

2. Please share and describe a paper that you have either read, written, or participated in writing that you believe exemplifies good writing. Discuss the attributes that make it a good paper.

3. What are the key elements of a problem statement? Can you provide two examples of problem statements from your own practice?

4. Every problem statement, when shared, helps you with reflecting in the revising process. Please tell us who are the audience you will share your problem statement with and how will their contributions help you revise it?

5. What is the motivation that drives your problem statement? Who will you collaborate with to do the root cause analysis of the problem statement you have developed?

## 8.8 | Assignment: Draft a Problem Statement

The assignment for this chapter is to draft a problem statement. You can choose one of two directions for your problem statement: (1) it can be practice-oriented or (2) research-oriented—for this assignment, we ask you to select one or the other, NOT both.

Revisit Section 8.3 and use this section as a reference of what goes into a narrative of a problem statement. As you start drafting your problem statement, use the outline you developed as part of the application section of this chapter. Remember, your problem statement should not be longer than 750 words, and you will probably need at least 500 words to unpack everything you need to unpack in a well-rounded problem statement.

## References

Chiang, I.A., Jhangiani, R.S., and Price, P.C. (2015). *Research Methods in Psychology* (2nd Ed.). BC Campus: Victoria, B.C. https://opentextbc.ca/researchmethods/

Purdue University. (n.d.). Purdue Online Writing Lab. https://owl.purdue.edu/owl/purdue_owl.html University of Southern California Libraries. (n.d.). Research Guides. https://libguides.usc.edu/writingguide/introduction/researchproblem

Scribber. (n.d.). How to Cite in APA Format (7th edition): Guide & Generator. https://www.scribbr.com/category/apa-style/

# CHAPTER 9

# Research Leading to Better Informed Practice: Action Research

*What research method provides tools for practical application that I can employ to investigate my own practice or use with a community of educators?*

## 9.1 | Introduction

### What Research Methods Provide Tools for Practical Application?

In the next three chapters, we present methods commonly employed by practitioners in the field of education. This chapter is the first of three discussing such methodologies. We start with the action research method. Arguably, action research is the most commonly used method in the field. Although not always obvious, much of what we do in education carries the elements of action research. For example, action research is widely employed in one's classroom to either perfect a content delivery method or try out a new pedagogical approach. In this chapter, we define what action research is, the basic assumptions of action research, the steps in action research, and how these steps may be applied in practice either by an individual professional or by a community of practice (a group of educators) to address a jointly agreed-upon problem of practice.

## 9.2 | Action Research

Action research is a commonly used term in the field, but if one were to assemble a group of educators, would they be able to define it? Or better yet, engage in action research?

> **Question** In a small group with three to four peers, discuss and take turns sharing your understanding/definition of action research. Take notes of your definitions and check the definitions you drafted against this text or as defined by your professor.

As we define what action research IS, it is equally important to know what action research is NOT.

**IS:** Although termed "research," which it is, action research IS more of a *process* that employs various methods during an investigation. While immersed in this process, the researcher positions them-self both as a researcher AND a participant as they examine their own practice and engage in inquiry (see Chapter 1). Action research IS systematic and employs various research methods in its process (e.g., qualitative, quantitative, mixed-method, survey, etc.). In other words, action research could utilize several methodologies. What IS critical in action research IS the process itself. Therefore, the process in action research must be carefully planned and follow a systematic step-by-step protocol.

Assumptions of action research in the field of education are as follows (Ferrance, 2000):

1. Teachers and principals work best on problems they have identified for themselves
2. Teachers and principals become more effective when encouraged to examine and assess their own work and then consider ways of working differently
3. Teachers and principals help each other by working collaboratively
4. Working with colleagues helps teachers and principals in their professional development
*(Watts, 1985, p. 118)*

**Purpose:** The purpose of employing action research is to inform one's professional practice through research and possibly introduce changes. Like many other research designs, action research must be purposeful where one must narrow down a topic and research questions first. The context is one of the essential elements of action research (after all, the entire purpose of action research is to study practice)! Context should be considered every step of the way, especially as a protocol to execute action research is designed.

**NOT:** Action research is NOT a traditional research project in a sense. It is NOT about doing research on/about people. Action research is NOT designed to find a correct answer but is a process of systematic steps to learn what improvements might be needed to improve one's practice. It is NOT designed to answer the *"why"* question (which is more common in research projects) but instead addresses the *"how"* question in practice. That is, *how* can we do things better within our professional context?

## Action Research: The Cyclical Nature and Steps

One of the distinct features of action research is that it is characterized by spiraling cycles. Each cycle includes topic selection, data collection, data analysis, problem formulation, data-driven action (from what is learned in previous steps), reflection on action taken and reexamination of the problem, possible problem redefinition with a purpose of engaging in another round of cycle, and so forth. This process involves three distinct areas (also see Figure 9.1): 1. **Investigation** (i.e., topic selection, data collection, and problem identification); 2. **Planning** (i.e., data analysis and problem formulation); 3. **Action** (i.e., data-driven action); and 4. **Reflection** (i.e., reflection on action taken and reexamination of the problem, possible problem redefinition). A professional or community of practice can engage in one cycle of action research or several. In a nutshell, action research is a cyclical process of trying out ideas in practice to improve that practice (Kemmis & McTaggart, 1988).

# Chapter 9: Research Leading to Better Informed Practice: Action Research

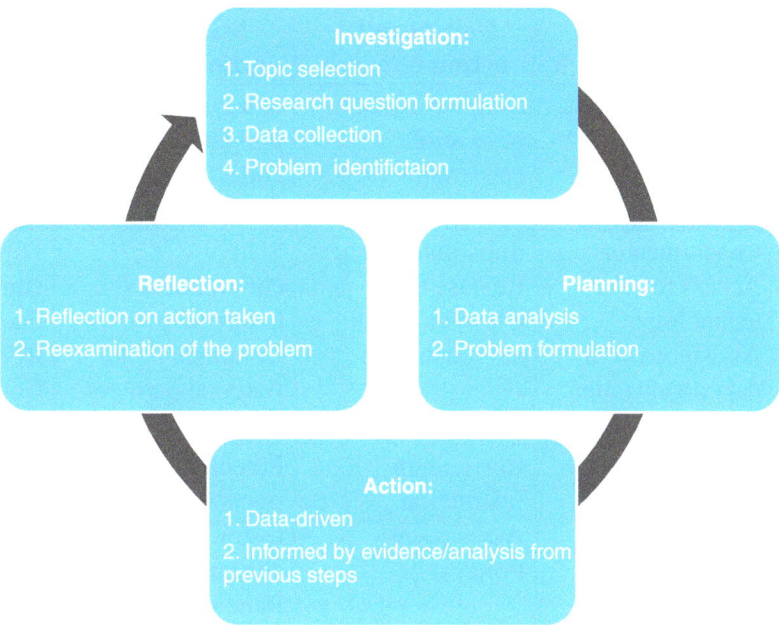

**Figure 9.1:** Steps in Action Research

## Types of Action Research

The handbook on action research assembled by Ferrance (2000) at Northeast and Islands Regional Educational Laboratory at Brown University presents a comprehensive overview of action research. We include Figure 9.2 from the handbook below for you to examine types of action research in education. Please notice that action research is often insular to an individual's profession but can also be extended to a community of practice, the entire school, or even the district!

> **Exercise** With your peer-review partner(s), go to the website where the handbook (Ferrance, 2000) on action research is located. Select one of the two "stories from the field" on pages 16 or 20. Read the story aloud and discuss takeaways and possible a way that you can engage in action research (considering your research topic/question) either individually or with a community of practice.

|  | Individual teacher research | Collaborative action research | School-wide action research | District-wide action research |
|---|---|---|---|---|
| **Focus** | Single classroom issue | Single classroom or several classrooms with common issue | School issue, problem, or area of collective interest | District issue Organizational structures |
| **Possible support needed** | Coach/mentor Access to technology Assistance with data organization and analysis | Substitute teachers Release time Close link with administrators | School commitment Leadership Communication External partners | District commitment Facilitator Recorder Communication External partners |
| **Potential Impact** | Curriculum Instruction Assessment | Curriculum Instruction Assessment Policy | Potential to impact school restructuring and change Policy Parent involvement Evaluation of programs | Allocation of resources Professional development activities Organizational structures Policy |
| **Side effects** | Practice informed by data Information not always shared | Improved collegiality Formation of partnerships | Improved collegiality, collaboration, and communication Team building Disagreements on process | Improved collegiality, collaboration, and communication Team building Disagreements on process Shared vision |

Figure 9.2: Types of Action Research and Uses

*Adapted from:* https://www.brown.edu/academics/education-alliance/sites/brown.edu.academics.education-alliance/files/publications/act_research.pdf

## 9.3 | Application: Action Research Through Instructional Leadership Inquiry Cycle

For this application assignment, we are asking you to step into the shoes of a school site leader/administrator and think through the four-step Instructional Leadership Inquiry Cycle.

Although the cyclical process of action research always follows the same progression, it is at times formulated differently for different professions or roles, even within the same field. For example, in the area of educational leadership, the focus of the process is always on the impact. Specifically, instructional leadership impacts on school culture, staff, students, and educational community as a whole.

As often the case, schools serve many functions to address their education community's needs. However, academic instruction is the primary function of any school. Therefore, the primary task of any school administrator is to provide instructional leadership and support instructional leaders at their sites. This said, school administrators and leaders often struggle with finding just the right approach to promote instructional excellence among their staff. Austin (2015) argues that effective administration and school leadership are complex processes requiring practice, expertise, and ongoing reflection of one's practice. For this reason, allotting time for a systemic inquiry into their instructional leadership practices is necessary for school leaders to be effective. Likewise, knowing where to start and what to do to engage in the inquiry is equally important (Austin, 2015). Hence a four-step process was developed to create Instructional Leadership Inquiry Cycle (see Figure 9.3).

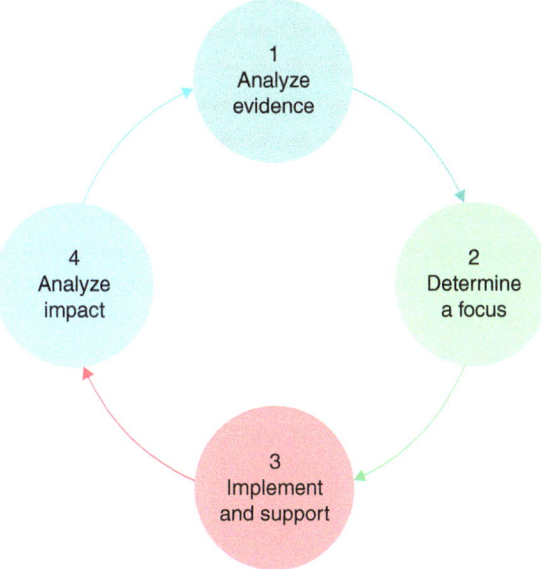

**Figure 9.3:** Instructional Leadership Inquiry Cycle
*Adapted from:* https://k-12leadership.org/4-steps-of-inquiry-that-help-principals-improve-instruction/

Where:

STEP 1: Analyzing evidence which includes multiple sources of data, such as standardized and other test scores, other assessments, classroom observations, and observation of school site leadership practices to narrow down the most pressing student learning problems and other contributing factors, such as instructional/pedagogical (teaching), and the problem of practice concerning leadership.

STEP 2: The focus should always be grounded in evidence and aligned with the site's/district's vision and mission for student achievement.

As leaders think through all the supports necessary to support the focus they determine, they must also think about the accountability systems, that is, how to hold staff accountable for implementing learning strategies.

STEP 3: The implement and support step's focus should always be to improve student learning in the identified area of need/focus as determined in the previous step. The step involves a balance between support and accountability with the following in mind: (1) planning individual support sessions with key staff to determine needs and resources; (2) planning for professional development activities; and (3) classroom observations.

STEP 4: The cycle of inquiry would not be complete without analyzing the impact of one's instructional leadership practices. In fact, this is the most critical segment of the cycle to determine (a) how effective the inquiry cycle is/was, (b) examine the short and long impact of the intervention, and (c) determine the next steps for engagement. Therefore, the following question should guide this step of engagement: *"What was learned about leadership practice and its impact on teacher practice and student learning? What are the implications for the next inquiry cycle?"* (Austin, 2015).

> **Exercise** Connect with two to three peers. It is best to engage in this application section with the support of a community of learners with whom you share interests. First, review and reflect on the steps of the leadership inquiry cycle and think through how you, as a community of learners/community of practice, might engage in the first two steps. Then, work collaboratively to analyze evidence you had collected previously (data from at least three school sites) and jointly determine what might be the areas of focus (no more than five) based on the evidence.

## 9.4 | Conclusion

In this first of three chapters designed to underline research methods in practice, we unpacked action research. Although not limited to the field of education, action research is the most applied in education. Everyone from teacher to administrator heard of this method and engaged in action research at some point in their career. Furthermore, this type of research and the cyclical nature of the application allows practitioners to revisit their own practices or that of a community of practice once or many times. All of which affords continuous improvement (at least in theory) of practice, which is a necessary *tool* to close the many existing and prevalent equity gaps within the educational system. Starting with one's own professional practice and expanding to a community of practice, school site and, even district will allow for reexamination, reevaluation, and improvement to take root.

## 9.5 | Discussion

1. As you reflect on your research engagements throughout this text and while using the instructional leadership inquiry cycle tool, what type of action research would you be interested in spearheading to narrow the equity gap? Think about our own professional practices as well as that of the school site community of practice.
2. What obstacles do you foresee if you were to attempt to utilize action research in your own classroom or with a community of educators/community of practice?

## 9.6 | Assignment

As a continuation of the exercise started in the application section with your peer group/community of learners, create an action research protocol based on the steps outlined in the Instructional Inquiry Leadership Cycle. Remember, you are stepping into a leadership/administrative role and should have concrete data from at least three school sites. Therefore, your community of learners effectively represents a leadership team of a small school district (leadership of three to four schools). Although you will be able to complete steps 1 and 2 with the information you have, do remember that this assignment is forward-looking. For steps 3 and 4, put your minds together in anticipation of outcomes and potential impact. That is, think through what supports might be needed during implementation and what might be the impact. This is a group assignment, so please remember to work collaboratively. And, most importantly, have fun working with data, determining focus, identifying supports, and anticipating impact!

## References

Austin, S. (2015). *4 steps of inquiry that help principals improve instruction.* https://k-12leadership.org/4-steps-of-inquiry-that-help-principals-improve-instruction/

Ferrance, E. (2000). *Action research.* Brown University: Providence, RI. https://repository.library.brown.edu/studio/item/bdr:qbjs2293/

Kemmis, S., & McTaggart, R. (1988). *The action research planner* (3rd ed.). Deakin University Press.

Watts, H. (1985). When teachers are researchers, teaching improves. *Journal of Staff Development, 6*(2), 118–127.

# CHAPTER 10
# Research Leading to Better Informed Practice: Survey Research

*Now that I completed my initial research and formulated a problem statement, how do I learn from my education community to make change possible and further engage in cycle of inquiry?*

## 10.1 | Introduction

This is the second of three chapters where we focus on research that is particularly useful in practice. In this chapter, we review and introduce foundational concepts in survey research. In education, a survey (or questionnaire) is a valuable and widespread tool to utilize in practice when wanting to learn more about the broader educational community, get insights from the staff, test a hypothesis, or even gather descriptive statistics for a widely dispersed sample. Along with the appropriate use of survey instruments and choosing a suitable methodology, you will learn about the strengths and weaknesses in survey research. Finally, in this chapter, we discuss basic tenets in the development and administration of a questionnaire.

## 10.2 | What Is Survey Research and Why Do I Need It?

Most if not all of us participated in taking surveys at some point in our lives. Whether we dreaded that time or were eager to share our opinions from the participant's end, **survey research** is a specific field in the research world. Focusing on methodologies and approaches to sampling, questionnaire development, and testing for validity and reliability, survey research is widely used for both practical application and in research. It is a particularly prevalent approach because one is able to collect large amounts of quantitative and qualitative information from a small or large sample relatively quickly (Ponto, 2015).

### A Survey

A well-designed survey can be an efficient and cost-effective tool to gather data about a population of interest by using a well-chosen sample design. If the sample is distributed randomly, researchers can make the assumption that the results are representative of the population of interest. Although it is true that a survey could be implemented in the context of a qualitative study, the power of representativeness of the sample would be compromised. In this chapter, we devote a section for qualitative considerations in using the survey instrument to unpack this further.

Surveys are usually cross-sectional by nature. This means that they represent a "snapshot" of the sample interviewed during a specific timeframe. These surveys are administered once and are great tools to gather attitudes, perceptions, knowledge, beliefs, and behaviors. Cross-sectional surveys reflect the point-in-time the data were collected and create no foundation for predictions or causation.

For example, one study wanted to test a hypothesis that adolescents who use their smartphones more often in the evenings would be associated with more daytime sleepiness for those adolescents (Nathan & Zeitzer, 2013). This study tested the hypothesis, but the results cannot be used to predict future associations—or even that increased phone use *caused* daytime sleepiness. The correct interpretation of the findings of the study were the associations found for that particular point-in-time.

If Nathan and Zeitzer (2013) were to administer the exact same questionnaire using the same methodology to a similar population, they would be able to start collecting "trend" data. **Trend data** is an important tool in education to assess areas that might need attention. For example, the California Healthy Kids Survey creates reports for each year of survey implementation at https://calschls.org.

> **Exercise** With your peer-review partner(s), examine the surveys from CalSchools by using the following link: https://calschls.org/survey-administration/downloads/#ssm_sc The website serves as a good resource by providing many surveys to be used as a *tool* by educators, school leaders, administrators, among others. After review, collaboratively select up to three surveys that you and your partner(s) would deem most applicable as these relate to your topic/population of focus. Examine these surveys and discuss how these could be implemented and what useful data the surveys you selected might generate to inform your topic further.

Surveys that are administered over time to the same respondents are called longitudinal surveys. Participants are often referred to as "cohorts" because they share a particular characteristic (like birth year). The National Longitudinal Surveys of Youth (NLSY) is an example of a cohort study that has been answering repeated measures in addition to new measures over multiple decades (Cooksey, 2017).

We discuss designing survey questions later in this chapter. But first, as researchers are quick to caution, before administration, a survey must be validated and reliable. *"What could be so hard about asking a few questions?"* you may ask, but in survey research, questions must be asked as written without deviation, the questionnaire must follow the prescribed order, and skip patterns must be observed. Any digressions introduce bias and researchers understand that bias equals error.

### *Strengths of Surveys*

Although the procedures and protocols around survey administration can be rigorous and stringent, these protocols are quite widespread for many good reasons. Because the surveys are standardized, there is little room for confusion in regard to items order. This facilitates the administration of the survey because training and quality control measures are more objectively assessed.

The cost of administering surveys can vary quite a bit, but it is certain that the costs are lower, and the breadth of data wider that could be captured in a semi-structured interview. Surveys also allow researchers and practitioners alike to reach respondents in a wider geographic area and provide a mechanism to reach respondents that might have particular characteristics that are difficult to find.

By using standardized surveys, researchers can often access standardized data dictionaries (which are technical guides to the instrument) and might even find some prepackaged statistical software code they can run to facilitate report writing of survey results. Most importantly, researchers who use questionnaires that have been validated and tested for reliability can be more secure in knowing they are measuring what they intend to measure accurately.

Chapter 10: Research Leading to Better Informed Practice: Survey Research  **105**

## *Weaknesses of Surveys*

Paradoxically, one positive feature regarding surveys and survey research is also a weaknesses. For example, the point made in the section above—that standardized surveys have a prescribed order and method of administration—does not allow for flexibility. Many of us have taken surveys where we wanted to answer "other," but the response categories did not allow for nuance or variation.

**Nonresponse**. Another weakness in surveys is the possibility that a researcher does not get enough responses to be able to state point estimates with enough certainty. Researchers need a certain number of responses to be able to make a statistical statement about the resulting data. If response rates are low, there may not be enough confidence that a result is "stable."

**Self-reported.** Respondents who report answers themselves may be influenced by a number of factors that cause them to report inaccurately. If the topic is sensitive, they may be embarrassed about answering. Respondents may be influenced by a "social desirability bias" and change an answer to please the interviewer (Althubaiti, 2016).

**Sample bias.** This type of error occurs when the respondents included in the survey do not accurately represent the population of interest (Ponto, 2015). This is the main reason researchers often randomize their samples. However sample bias can occur in many other ways: not translating an instrument when a second language is prevalent in the population of interest; calling during business hours when respondents are at work; using complicated language, or complex skip (contingency) patterns, and so on.

> **Exercise** Based on what you learned about surveys thus far, engage in the following self-reflective questions: (1) What other types of error can you imagine when developing or administering a survey? (2) Why do you think surveys are a widely used research method in education? (3) Do you like to answer surveys? Why/why not?

## 10.3 | Steps in Survey Research

Survey research is not so clear-cut as to say there are linear steps to a successful implementation. Developing a survey and administering it can sound deceptively easy. However, there are many considerations in the process. In this section, we highlight the most salient activities in launching a survey based on your selected topic and population of focus (application and assignments from earlier engagements).

### Selecting a Sample

When selecting a sample, among your very first decisions should be whether you are planning to use a probability or nonprobability sample. In education, there are plenty of appropriate uses for each strategy. If you would like to be able to generalize your study findings to the bigger population, and you know each member of the population will have some chance of being selected, you will likely choose a probability sample. However, some researchers may not "know" the entire population and, therefore, cannot implement a probabilistic sample selection. For this scenario, a nonprobability sample is likely the correct choice. There are several types of sampling strategies. Figure 10.1 gives an overview of commonly used strategies. A brief discussion of each strategy follows.

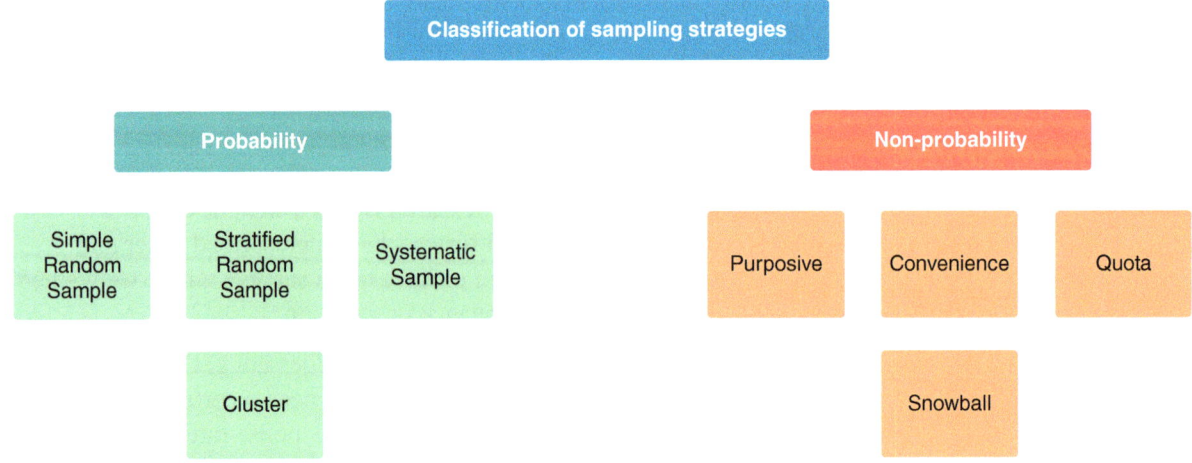

**Figure 10.1** Classification of Sampling Strategies

## Probability Sample

**Simple Random Sample.** This is a popular method when the researcher knows the population to choose from: for example, all K-12 principals in California public schools. There are many computer programs, including Excel, that will randomize a sample list to contact. This sample list is often called a "sampling frame." Students will recall that sample is randomized to avoid bias—the idea is that a researcher is literally randomizing error to create results that are generalizable to the larger population because each member has an opportunity to be selected as part of the sample.

**Stratified Random Sample.** This is a good method when you know there are certain categories you want to be sure you capture in proportion to the population. Using the example above—perhaps you know the population of principals includes 60% males and 40% females. As a researcher, you may want to be certain you get a proportional sample because gender is an important part of your research question. In this situation, you would divide the population list into two: one for male principals and one for female principals. After that, you randomly select sample in proportion to your population of interest.

**Systematic Sample.** With this strategy, you may have a smaller population list. Starting with a random number, a researcher can select every "$n^{th}$" member of the list, depending on the size of the sample needed.

**Cluster Sample.** This is a commonly used strategy in school-based education research. In this scenario, the "population of interest" might be a cluster: a classroom, a school, a district, and so on. The population list would then be the universe of classrooms, schools, or districts and the sample would be drawn from those clusters.

## Nonprobability Sample

**Purposive Sample.** With this strategy, the main concern is not representativeness or proportionality, but rather, a researcher would like to survey a member of the population with a particular characteristic. For example, principals who are over 65 and still serving as administrators. There is likely not a population list to choose from, and a research wants to find out information from those that meet the established criteria.

**Convenience Sample.** In some situations, researchers want to collect information quickly without knowing the population of interest. We can envision this type of sampling in malls where market researchers ask opinions of passersby. In education, researchers might use this method to collect opinions or attitudes of students.

**Quota Sample.** This is different than stratified random sample in that all members of the population are not known. The researcher, however, wants to make sure they interview a certain number of certain categories of the population of interest. An example would be that a researcher might be interested in learning about the opinions of teachers about Critical Race Theory. The researcher wants to be certain they interview a certain number of teachers from various race groups that are proportional to the school, therefore "quotas." Another large distinction from stratified random sample, is that you interview anyone that meets your quota, without regard to random probability.

**Snowball Sample.** This sampling strategy is particularly useful when you do not know how many "candidates" exist in a population. For example, if you are interested in doing research on transgender principals. It is called "snowball" or "respondent generated sample" because you ask your respondent to refer you to other people that meet the study criteria. Because there is likely no existing list of transgender principals, you may need to rely on your respondents to point you in the right direction to find additional participants.

## Sample Size: How Many Is Enough? *It Depends!*

The most common question that comes up in practice and research is whether one needs to survey everyone or a select sample to know with a certain degree of confidence whether responses apply to the population, for example, education community at a school site, teachers in a district, and so on. The answer is "depends"—that is, it depends on the confidence level and margin of error you are/a research is comfortable with (or possible to achieve) and the size of your population. If the size of your population is small, then it is likely that you will need to survey everyone in order to know whether responses are generalizable to your population of focus. But, if the size of your population is considerable or let us say more than 80, then a probability sample of a certain size should give you a solid picture of the entire population.

**Table 10.1:** Sample Size for Validity. *Number of returned, useable surveys needed are based on the size of the target population and on confidence level and confidence interval desired.*

**Adapted from:** https://www.extension.uidaho.edu/publishing/pdf/bul/bul0870.pdf

| Confidence interval | | Confidence Level | Size of Target Population | | | | | |
|---|---|---|---|---|---|---|---|---|
| | | | 100 | 1,000 | 5,000 | 10,000 | 50,000 | 100,000 |
| ±4% | | 90% | 81 | 298 | 392 | 408 | 422 | 424 |
| | | 95% | 86 | 375 | 536 | 566 | 593 | 597 |
| | | 99% | 91 | 509 | 859 | 939 | 1,016 | 1,026 |
| ±5% | | 90% | 73 | 214 | 258 | 265 | 271 | 272 |
| | | 95% | 79 | 278 | 357 | 370 | 381 | 383 |
| | | 99% | 87 | 399 | 586 | 622 | 655 | 659 |

Table 10.1 provides a general guideline of how many samples from a target population are needed to be able to draw generalizable conclusions. These numbers are calculated based on a statistical formula as outlined below (Parten, 1950).

$$n = \frac{NZ^2 * 0.25}{d^2 * (N-1) + (Z^2 * 0.25)}$$

Where

$n$ = The sample size required and which is statistically representative (the number that we aim to find)

$N$ = The target population size

$d$ = Confidence level (0.05)

$Z$ = Number of standard deviation units of the sampling distribution corresponding to the desired confidence level given as 1.96 (at 95% confidence level).

If you suddenly got scared by all the statistics, do not despair! There are online tools that calculate the target population sample for you. The one we often use in class (after we have our students engage in calculating by hand—it is easier than you think! And, fun too—a skill of sorts) is from the online survey tool called "SurveyMonkey," which allows one to enter the population size, confidence level, and percentage of error you are comfortable with. Do note that the rule of thumb (a good practice, in other words) is to select at least a 95% confidence level and a 5% margin of error. When engaging in an interactive exercise below, you will notice that the SurveyMonkey online tool is preset to the 95/5 guideline.

> **Exercise** Based on your topic of interest and research question, determine whom (we suggest choosing either teachers OR students, as appropriate) you might need to survey to add to the knowledge on your chosen topic. Next, look up the number of teachers or students in your selected population for your school site and then district. After use the following link/tool: https://www.surveymonkey.com/mp/sample-size-calculator/ to calculate how many responses you would need to ensure that survey is generalizable for the size of your target population at 95/5 levels. Once you obtain these numbers and based on your knowledge, what else you must consider with respect to stratification to ensure accurate representation of responses, especially at the district level?

## Preparing the Instrument

As discussed earlier in this chapter, when administering a survey, it is always best to select an instrument that has already been validated and found to be reliable. With this in mind, whether you are using a validated survey or the one you recently designed to survey your education community, you will need to create an easy-to-navigate instrument for respondents. If a written questionnaire, use simple graphics and clear instructions. If a web survey, use clear instructions and avoid having to endlessly scroll, and so on.

If you are unable to find an appropriate existing instrument and you decide to develop your own questionnaire, make sure you ask clear questions with distinct (mutually exclusive) response categories. Avoid asking two questions when you expect one answer. Sometimes referred to as "double-barreled" questions: they might seem clear to the researcher, but confusing to the respondent/participant. One example of a "double-barreled" question is, *"Are you satisfied with your salary and the support you get from the principal?"*—there are clearly two questions in one and would merit two different answers.

Another factor to consider when developing questions is the type of analysis you want to perform. Closed-ended questions limit responses to certain choices only and lend themselves to more of a quantitative analysis. Open-ended questions allow the respondent to create a response that is not predetermined—these also allow for the collection of more nuanced responses and often lend themselves to more of a qualitative analytic strategy.

| Closed-ended | Open-ended |
|---|---|
| Pros | Pros |
| • Consistency of responses are enhanced across respondents | • Allow more freedom of response |
| • Easier and faster to tabulate | • Easier to construct |
| • More popular with respondents-less cognitively taxing | • Capture more nuance and detail |
| Cons | Cons |
| • May limit extent of response information | • Responses may be inconsistent in length and content across respondents |
| • Take more time to construct and test | • Both questions and responses subject to misinterpretation |
| • May require more questions to cover the research topic | • Harder to tabulate, code, and synthesize |

Figure 10.2 Question Types: Pros and Cons

No matter whether you use an existing survey or create your own, always be sure to pretest your questionnaire. If you developed your own questions, be sure to test those for understandability by administering your survey to a small group of likely respondents. Many researchers and practitioners skip this step to their own detriment. It is a very disappointing feeling to realize you lost data because your questionnaire contained an error in the instructions, or because your programming was incorrectly constructed.

An important step in your scripting is to ensure there are clear and simple instructions along with well thought-out introductions to each section. If you are creating a written survey for respondents to fill out themselves, make sure you prepare a compelling cover letter that stresses the importance of the survey and for the survey studies includes important human subjects review information and/or confidentiality statements (is surveys are used for the purposes of soliciting feedback from colleagues/staff).

## 10.4 | Application

### Peer-Activity: Design a Survey Based on Topic of Interest

Now it is time to apply your survey research knowledge! Select a topic from Figure 10.3 that aligns (closely or broadly) with your own topic of interest and/or population of focus. Then go to the website and download the survey. After examining the survey, design a short questionnaire that would take participants five to ten minutes to complete—the questionnaire/survey can include questions that have already been fielded from the survey you examined. In addition, please create your own questions that would include at least one of each type of the following questions: A question that would lead to "Yes"/ "No" answer; a multiple-choice question; a question requiring a numeric response; and an open-ended question. As you develop this brief survey, reflect on the challenges you faced with the questions you created. You will be sharing your survey with your peers as part of the assignment exercise (see Section 10.7)

> Examples of large surveys in education:
>
> The National Household Education Surveys Program (NHES) provides descriptive data on the educational activities of the U.S. population and offers researchers, educators, and policymakers a variety of statistics on the condition of education in the United States. https://nces.ed.gov/nhes
>
> The Adult Training and Education Survey (ATES) provides data on work-related credentials held by adults in the United States and how adults prepared for those credentials. Related to adult education, it will provide information on participation in basic education and occupational courses or training, as well as credentials obtained, among adults who do not have a high school diploma or equivalent. https://www.air.org/project/adult-training-and-education-survey-ates
>
> The Panorama Teacher Survey is designed to spark and support productive conversations between teachers and school leaders about professional learning, school communication, school climate, and other key topics. https://www.panoramaed.com/panorama-teacher-survey
>
> The Youth Risk Behavior Surveillance System (YRBSS) monitors six categories of health-related behaviors that contribute to the leading causes of death and disability among youth and adults, including: Behaviors that contribute to unintentional injuries and violence; sexual behaviors related to unintended pregnancy and sexually transmitted diseases; alcohol and other drug use; tobacco use; unhealthy dietary behaviors; and inadequate physical activity. https://www.cdc.gov/healthyyouth/data/yrbs/index.htm

**Figure 10.3** Example of Surveys in Education

> **Resource** Educational needs assessments are necessary to learn about important issues and problems faced by a population/public to design effective educational programs. Needs assessments, are therefore, can serve as an essential tool for sound practice. We provide a link to the source that unpacks the methods for conducting a needs assessment; we encourage you to review the document and think of ways to include needs assessments in practice. https://www.extension.uidaho.edu/publishing/pdf/bul/bul0870.pdf

## 10.5 | Discussion

1. Based on your current and future career aspirations, what are some of the best ways to utilize surveys?
2. Do surveys have the ability to tell you everything? What do they tell you?
3. What are some of the pitfalls of "self-reported" data?
4. Provide an example from your work as an educator where administering a survey will give you more actionable information than focus groups or structured interviews?
5. Describe a survey done in your area of interest that you were involved in or read about? Please describe its purpose, the participants who participated in the survey, and where and when the findings were reported?

## 10.6 | Conclusion

We hope that you found this chapter useful and, more importantly, applicable to your particular area of the field. Our aim was to provide an overview of salient topics in survey research as they apply to education research and add to your research toolkit. There are many researchers who spend entire careers looking at topics in questionnaire development, question order, cognitive testing, analytic considerations, and survey performance overtime. And, although we cannot possibly cover every aspect of survey research, we did provide the most useful basics that you can use as tools as you continue to build your competency and literacy in understanding research.

## 10.7 | Assignment: Peer-collaboration and Survey Feedback

**Part A.** Take surveys created by two of your peers. As you take the survey, take notes on the structure of questions, the feelings you might have as participants about the questions and their order, and so on. Then, share your notes/written feedback with each of your peers, being sure to comment on germane items that were discussed in this chapter. For example, you may touch on question construction; was there an item you did not know how to answer? Was there a confusing item? Or a double-barreled question?

**Part B**. What feedback did you receive about your survey—was there anything you would change? What do you think about the data you collected from your peers? Did you find you collected data of interest? Would you have added more questions? Would you be more likely to take a survey the next time you are asked to complete one? As an educational leader/school administrator, would you be more likely to allow a survey in your school district? Or, less likely and why?

## References

Althubaiti, A. (2016). Information bias in health research: Definition, pitfalls, and adjustment methods. *Journal of Multidisciplinary Healthcare, 9,* 211–217. https://doi.org/10.2147%2FJMDH.S104807

Cooksey, E. C. (2017, November 21). *Using the National Longitudinal Surveys of Youth (NLSY) to conduct life course analyses.* Springer. https://www.ncbi.nlm.nih.gov/books/NBK543729/

Nathan, N., & Zeitzer, J. (2013). A survey study of the association between mobile phone use and daytime sleepiness in California high school students. *BMC Public Health, 13*(1). https://doi.org/10.1186/1471-2458-13-840

Parten, M. (1950). *Surveys, Polls, and Samplings: Practical Procedure.* New York: Harper and Brothers.

Ponto, J. (2015). Understanding and evaluating survey research. *Journal of the Advanced Practitioner in Oncology, 6,* 168–171. https://www.ncbi.nlm.nih.gov/pmc/articles/PMC4601897/

# CHAPTER 11

# Research Leading to Better Informed Practice: Single-Case Research

*What research method provides tools for practical application that I can use to learn whether an intervention is effective?*

## 11.1 | Introduction

This is the last of three chapters specifically focused on research methods that professionals find helpful to improve practice. In this chapter, we focus on a single-case research, which is often used in Special Education. This said, single-case research is not limited to one area of education or other fields. Psychology and human behavior fields, in particular, regularly employ single-case research design. Our goal for this chapter is to provide an overview of the single-case design, its foundational underpinnings, and its uses. We then engage you in the application of knowledge, followed by a discussion and assignment. We hope that the information and engagements in this chapter prove useful and further expand your toolkit in using research as a tool.

## 11.2 | Single-Case Research

As we define single-case research, we would like to acknowledge that there are several designs under the umbrella of single-case research. In this chapter, we cover single-case designs that are most frequently used in the field of education. We start with an overview of the general characteristics of single-case research and then go over the specific features shared between single-case research designs. After, we unpack a few specific designs to model how these might be used in practice.

> "Single-Case Research is a method to evaluate and test the success or failure of an intervention on a case."

### An Overview

> "A case is a person/individual, school, or community"

The following question: *Why a researcher or practitioner would employ single-case research?* would help us both look into the *why* and discuss *how* single-case research is applied. But first, let us take a closer look at what it is. **Single-case** research is a method to evaluate and test the success or failure of an intervention on a case. **A case** could be a person/individual, school, or community. The overarching goal of single-case research is to provide evidence of how effective an intervention is while using a relatively small sample size or a sample size of one.

Researchers and practitioners employ single-case research to examine a single case or a limited number of cases (sharing similar characteristics) that present unique behaviors needing intervention. Although most frequently used in the areas of special education and counseling within the field of education, single-case research can be used in other contexts of the field. The main characteristic of a single-case research is that it allows researchers to examine individual differences compared to studies that examine populations and focus on the average outcomes.

Contexts or situations where a participant might present an interesting or challenging case of specific needs requiring intervention would qualify to employ single-case research. It is important to note that in addition to examining the impact of an intervention on behavior, single-case research can be used to examine learning outcomes. For example, if a teacher wishes to change an individual student's behavior or that of a group of students by implementing an intervention to test and document the effectiveness of such intervention, single-case research would be an appropriate method to employ. Or, in a case of a student with special needs requiring individualized learning intervention specific to their need, the effectiveness of the intervention is critical in determining the next steps to support that student's academic achievement. Or in a case of an administrator desiring to build trust and buy-in with their new-to-the-profession teacher to ensure risk-safe teaching evaluation and receptivity of feedback. The list goes on. As you can see, single-case research can be quite valuable in practice.

## Shared Characteristics Across Single-Case Research Designs

First, single-case research generally employs observations through visual analysis of behaviors by systematically comparing a participant(s) behavior before they receive an intervention to the same behaviors during an intervention and, finally, after the intervention. To document, the baseline and patterns of behavior changes (or the lack thereof). The patterns and changes are documented in the form of a line graph to determine the effect of the introduced intervention. This style of documentation provides clear evidence of how effective or ineffective an intervention is (Kazdin, 2021). Later, in this section, we present several graphs as examples when we discuss specific designs.

Second, it is important to understand what goes into single-case research and the essential features shared between designs. These foundational features are as follows: (a) baseline data to establish prediction; (b) continues and repeated measurement and manipulation of independent and dependent variables to establish verification; and (c) replication of the intervention and its effect on the participant—this needs to be done over time so the participant would essentially serve as their own control—this is one of the most essential features of the single-case research, that is, each case also serves as its control, and, therefore, eliminating the need for a control group Therefore, replication of intervention is the key to showing effectiveness (Kazdin, 2021).

Third, single-case research adheres to few basics:

**The dependent variable** (always represented on the *y*-axis) in single-case research **is the observation of behavior** prior (to establish a baseline), during (to observe the intended outcome of the intervention), and after treatment. Thus, it should be measured repeatedly and be consistent within and across conditions.

**The independent variable** (represented by the *x*-axis) is the intervention itself. Theoretically, the intervention should produce changes in behavior or other outcomes (dependent variable) that are observable. In single-case research, independent variables are actively manipulated; therefore, it is important to decide when intervention is introduced and withdrawn to document its effectiveness accurately.

**Baseline** is the usual behavior without intervention and before introducing a treatment. The baseline behavior (dependent variable) is measured over time (five to seven days) until a consistent response pattern is present.

**Conditions** are often assigned a designated letter A, B, C, and so on.

**Change in conditions** is not dependent upon time or a fixed number of observations, but rather participant's behavior. Therefore, a researcher waits for the change of behavior before moving to another condition or introducing/reintroducing treatment. The important element in single-case research observations is consistency. Once a condition becomes consistent, that usually serves as a signal to move on to the next condition. This approach is called "steady state strategy" (Sidman, 1960). The idea behind the steady state strategy is for the dependent variable to reach the steady state. When the dependent variable reaches a steady state within a condition, then the change or variations across conditions are very relatively to detect.

## Single-Case Research Designs: AB, ABA, BAB, and Multiple Baseline Design

The first three designs that we will cover are AB, ABA, and BAB. To better understand (and convey) their practical application is to illustrate each one through graphical representation. We use the same intervention through all three examples for consistency purposes.

**AB:** Let us assume that we want to investigate the effect of positive redirection feedback on unwanted behavior over a period of time. First, we would need to establish a baseline through observation of how frequently the unwanted behavior occurs and consistently record the number of episodes. Figure 11.1 displays the baseline, which we term "A."

After establishing a baseline with consistent pattern over time (in our case, it is five days), we can then begin an intervention. As a reminder, the intervention is our independent variable (represented in the *x*-axis); in this case, our intervention is positive redirection feedback. Figure 11.1 illustrates the frequency of unwanted behavior (B) after the intervention.

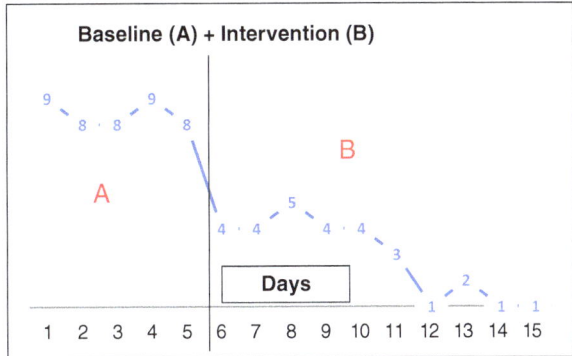

**Figure 11.1:** Documentation of Baseline (A) + Intervention (B)

We can see that the frequency of unwanted behavior has decreased after the intervention and can conclude that feedback on disruptive behavior was effective. This example follows the AB single-subject design, where A is an established baseline and B is an intervention.

**ABA (also called a reversal design):** Now, let us assume that we want to see whether the unwanted behavior returns after we withdraw the feedback and, more importantly, to check on whether the change in behavior is due to our treatment and not other factors. Our next step is to withdraw the treatment and return to the baseline observation (A). This reversal greatly increases the internal validity of the single-case study.

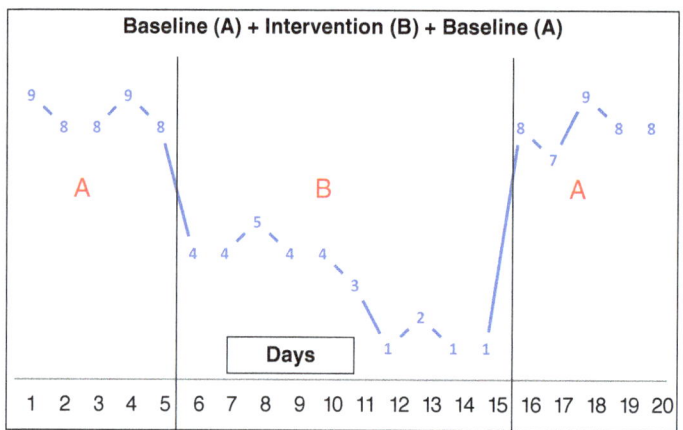

**Figure 11.2:** Documentation of Baseline (A) + Intervention (B) + Baseline (A)

In this particular case (Figure 11.2), we can observe that intervention did impact unwanted behavior. To determine whether this particular intervention is successful, we would need to replicate the intervention.

**BAB:** There are times when an intervention is of an urgent matter. Therefore, a researcher or practitioner does not have the luxury of time to document the baseline before introducing intervention. In such cases, intervention is introduced without documenting the initial baseline. The intervention is then followed by a period without intervention, followed by the reintroduction of intervention.

> "A baseline is established for several participants and the treatment is then introduced to each participant at a different time." (Chiang, Jhangiani, & Price, 2015).

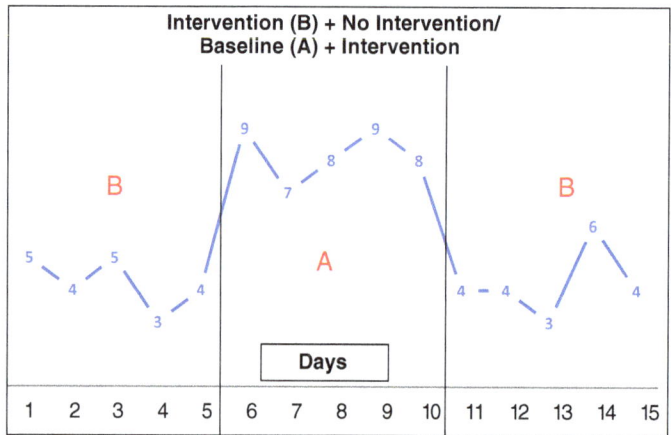

**Figure 11.3:** Documentation of Intervention (B) + Baseline (A) + Intervention (B)

Again, in this example, the intervention appears to make a difference and unwanted behavior returns when intervention is withdrawn.

These withdrawal and reversal designs (AB, ABA, etc.) can continue in this pattern. In order for the design to provide evidence that the intervention was indeed effective, a researcher needs to rely on the evidence of behavior reversal during the withdrawal period as shown above through AB, ABA, and BAB.

## Multiple Baseline Design

Multiple baseline designs are necessary due to several issues that might arise with AB, ABA, and so forth designs. One, a removal of intervention that is working sometimes can be harmful to the participant; therefore, a removal of that intervention would be unethical. Another reason would be that the dependent variable might not return to the baseline since either the treatment has had an impact that is sustaining or something else is at play that made a difference in behavior. Therefore, multiple baseline design is necessary.

A baseline is established for several participants in a multiple baseline design, and each of the participants is tested in the AB design pattern when treatment is introduced. The central component of this design is that the treatment is spread out and introduced at different times to each participant by staggering the start of intervention while at the same time assessing the baseline performance of those participants who have not yet experienced intervention. Consequently, intervention and baseline behaviors are then compared to determine whether an intervention had an impact. Multiple baseline designs can be used to demonstrate intervention effects with:

1. Additional participants (across individuals).
2. Additional problems for the same participant (across behaviors).
3. Same problem and same participant in different settings (across settings).

*Example*: Three women are referred to a program, each of whom reports suffering from overeating behaviors. Baseline data is gathered for each participant, but the length of the baseline period varies across the participants. Participant 1 begins treatment, and data collection continues for all three women, whereas the second and third women continue to remain in the baseline period. The second woman does not begin treatment until there is a clear indication that the first woman who is receiving treatment experiences a reduction in her overeating behaviors. Similarly, the third woman does not begin treatment until the second woman experiences a reduction in her behaviors. Repeated measurement would continue for all three women throughout the process, but the second and third women would have a longer baseline period than the first.

If the treatment is the sole determinant of improvement, then behavior should change only when the treatment is implemented and not before. Therefore, participants who remain in the baseline phase should not show behavior change until they themselves have been treated. In the example above, if the treatment is directly related to overeating behavior reduction, the effect should be evident in the data from all three participants. Specifically, overeating behaviors in the second and third women would continue at the baseline level until the onset of treatment.

Figure 11.4 illustrates the relationship between a dependent variable and an independent variable in a multiple baseline design with three participants. In this example, Participant 1 received the intervention at week six, Participant 2 received the intervention at week 10, and Participant 3 received the intervention at week 14. Although the baseline phase varied in length for each participant, a trend in behavior was present across participants, as evident by the stability of behavior during this period. Once the intervention was introduced, another pattern of behavior emerged at the onset of the intervention phase.

From: SINGLE-CASE DESIGN BRIEF

https://www.jbassoc.com/wp-content/uploads/2018/03/Selecting-Single-Case-Designs.pdf

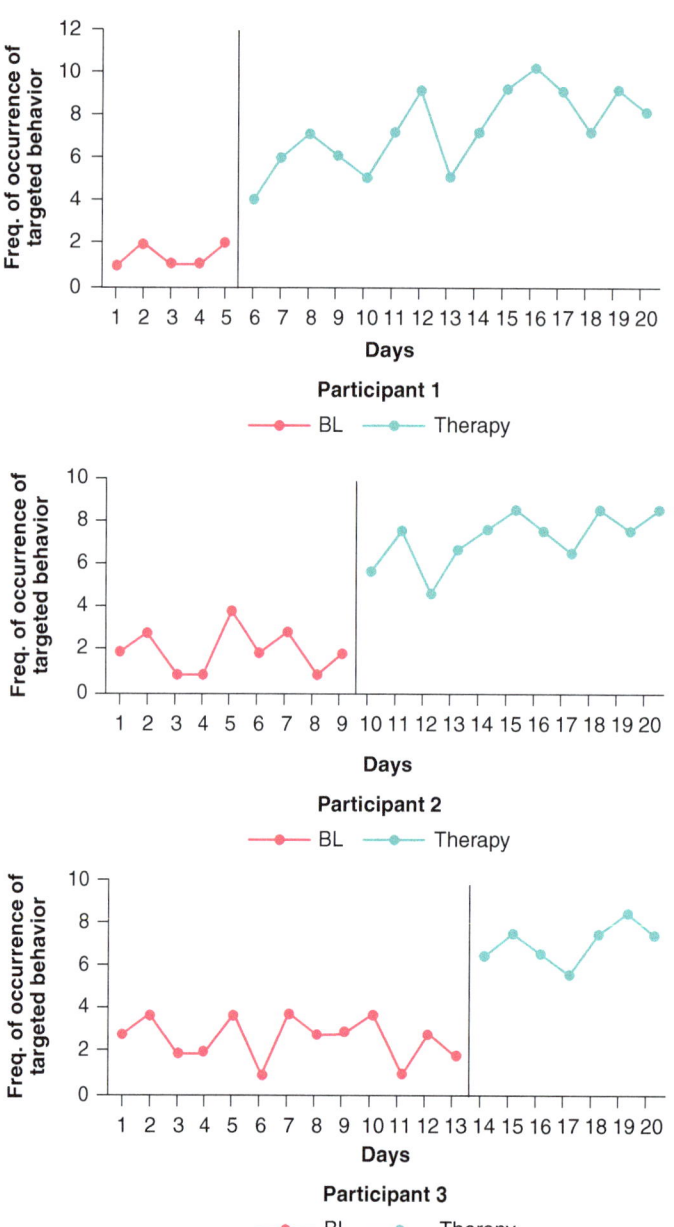

Figure 11.4: Example of Multiple Baseline Design With Three Participants

## 11.3 | Application

Perhaps, one of the most well-known single-case studies in education is *Bully Prevention in Positive Behavior Support* by Ross and Horner (2009). This study was specifically designed to change practice by introducing intervention in bully prevention utilizing multiple baseline design. We believe that examining this study and learning from it will provide several ideas for how to use single-case design as a tool in your own practice.

Therefore, and as part of this application engagement, we would like you to familiarize yourselves with this study and its methods. First, read the article, which can be found by selecting the following link: https://www.ncbi.nlm.nih.gov/pmc/articles/PMC2791686/pdf/jaba-42-04-747.pdf. Then examine the discussion section and, more so, implications for practice and limitations. What are some of the take-aways from the implication for practice section for you? In what ways do these implications apply to your school site of focus? Finally, after reading the limitations section, what are some ways these limitations could be overcome?

## 11.4 | Conclusion

Similar to other methodologies, the evolution of methods is expected and desired over time since, without evolution, there is no progress. Single-case experimental designs are no exception. However, perhaps, the greatest strength of single-case research is that it can draw strong causal inferences. This has been observed to be evident in both experimental and applied areas of research (Kazdin, 2021). Therefore, single-case research and designs have the strengths for much greater use, especially in application and practice contexts and not limited to a limited number of areas in education. As educators, education leaders, and aspiring administrators, we genuinely hope you take advantage of single-case research and apply it in practice.

## 11.5 | Discussion

1. As you reflect on ways single-case research can be used in practice, think about and describe an instance where interaction over an extended period of time with one student (or a small group of students sharing characteristics) has had implications on you as an educator. Were there any interventions or possible routine that you introduced during the course of your interaction? If so, how did that impact student's trajectory?
2. Reflecting on your professional trajectory, think of ways and areas where a single-case study (an intervention) is needed to impact practice. Specifically, think about what it would take, discuss the length of study, area of focus, purpose, and an anticipated impact of the study.
3. What is the value added of a single-case study as compared to research encompassing a large sample?
4. What are the limitations of single-case studies?

## 11.6 | Assignment

Now that you had an opportunity to learn about single-case research and read one of the studies employing multiple single-case design (Section 11.3), circle back to your topic and population of focus and think of a possible single-case design intervention that could potentially improve student academic performance and/or well-being. Remember, single-case design studies focus on a case where a case could be a person/individual, a small group of individuals sharing characteristics, school, or community. Next, draft a roadmap/plan for a single-case intervention. Remember to include proposed intervention(s) and the intended impact of such interventions. This roadmap/plan should be concise (no more than a page) and align with your interests/topic to further advance your inquiry and provide additional ways for solutions to address the identified equity gap.

## References

Chiang, I. A., Jhangiani, R. S., & Price, P. C. (2015). *Research methods in psychology* (2nd ed.). Victoria, BC: BC Campus. https://opentextbc.ca/researchmethods/chapter/single-subject-research-designs/#return-footnote-955-2

Kazdin, A. E. (2021). https://onlinelibrary.wiley.com/doi/epdf/10.1002/jeab.638

Ross, S. W., & Horner, R. H. (2009). Bully prevention in positive behavior support. *Journal of Applied Behavior Analysis 2009, 42*, 747–759. https://www.ncbi.nlm.nih.gov/pmc/articles/PMC2791686/pdf/jaba-42-04-747.pdf

Sidman, M. (1960). *Tactics of scientific research: Evaluating experimental data in psychology.* Authors Cooperative.

# CHAPTER 12

# Well-Informed Decisions Lead to Better Outcomes: Research as a Tool for Educators, Education Leaders, and Administrators

## 12.1 | Introduction

At last, we are on our final chapter! But first, we would like to recap your trajectory with us. On your journey, you learned about inquiry, the scientific method, as well as the basics of how to read research (Chapters 1 and 2). You chose a topic and population of interest while focusing on the state's priorities/indicators (Chapters 2 and 3). You learned how to search for and collect literature about your topic and construct an annotated bibliography (Chapter 3). While studying about quantitative methods, you engaged in the descriptive examination of data with a school site in mind (Chapter 4). And, as you learned about qualitative methods, you designed protocols for qualitative data collection (Chapter 5). After all this, you arrived at learning about sequential mixed methods and discovered that engaging quantitative and qualitative data affords a more robust and in-depth investigation (Chapter 6). While analyzing the many layers of data, you gained knowledge about coding qualitative data and deriving themes to further inform quantitative findings (Chapter 7). Having a grasp on the basics of APA style as outlined in Chapter 8 will serve you well for years to come—although tedious at a first glance, using the style of our field (APA) will soon become effortless In constructing your problem statement, you got to practice ways of conceptualization while contextually framing the equity gap identified earlier/as part of your equity gap analysis. Perhaps, messy at first, writing a convincing problem statement about an issue you attempt to solve will enable the necessary stakeholder buy-in to change the education system by addressing existing and prevalent equity gaps (Chapter 8). While at it, you examined and engaged in applying other research methods that serve as impactful tools in practice; for example, action research, survey research, and single-case research (Chapters 9, 10, and 11). What a journey! There is only one thing left before we part, a culminating assignment. We unpack the two directions below.

## 12.2 | Circling Back to What *IS*

Let us be reminded about what education, specifically Early Childhood (EC) to grade 12 education is all about and what EC-12 education represents to three distinct groups: (a) consumers of education (students and, indirectly, parents), (b) those who are in charge of content delivery (teachers and instructional support staff), and (c) those who oversee both consumption and delivery of education (administrators).

> **Food for Thought** Thinking of the three groups listed above (i.e., students and parents; teachers/instructional support staff; and school administrators), how do you think each would define what education *IS*?

As we part, we would like you to remember that the field of education is a service field: service to the students, their families, and communities. Without the students attending our schools, there would be no need for teachers and instructional support staff, school administrators, district administrators, professors teaching this class, and so on. The students are the *why*. Therefore, and as we reflect on the systems that shape education and academic/life trajectories for the students/our students, we must consider their needs, especially the unique and diverse needs they bring to a classroom. This consideration is particularly important since it is our job and basic obligation to address students' needs first and foremost to make education possible. So, what does it take? you may ask.

Simply put, it takes well-informed, well-skilled professionals. There is little doubt that well-informed teachers and administrators who employ decision-making grounded in evidence, leads to better outcomes for the students *for whom* and, importantly, *because of whom* the education system exists. Whether in practice or research, in a classroom or the district office, the tools and methods we use to conceptualize, anticipate, and construct a plan for improvement in addressing problems and providing solutions make all the difference.

Educators, education leaders, and school administrators who know how to utilize data to establish evidence and engage in research are (simply put) better informed, and therefore are more effective at decision-making, while having a greater impact on their students and education communities they serve. They are able to readily and easily align the strategies for improvement to their education community's needs and, as a result, easily and (at times but not always) effortlessly establish buy-in from their stakeholders.

## 12.3 | Application: Practice and Research

As you approach your culminating assignment for the course, in this section, we ask that you start conceptualizing/thinking about an outline for school improvement strategies or, alternatively, drafting a research proposal for a larger study/project. We ask that you select one or the other direction and not both.

We unpack the details for practical and research application here to get you thinking on a path of next steps. We then provide templates for both in the assignment section and ask that you complete one as a culminating assignment.

> —A goal is defined as a *"desired result or outcome"* over a specified time
>
> —An objective is *"how you will get there"*
>
> —objectives succinctly describe activities involved in achieving a goal

### Planning Strategies for School Improvement

If you selected practical application option as your culminating experience, constructing strategies for school improvement is your next step. Based on your topic and evidence you collected thus far (see prior assignments) as well as the problem statement, create an outline for ***three*** and no more than five evidence-based strategies to address the equity gap that you identified earlier through data analysis (see Chapter 7 assignment). In doing so, reflect on the problem statement and necessary buy-in from the stakeholders. As you brainstorm, think about the following:

1. What is your vision for the strategy and how this aligns with the school's vision? How would you define success? What are you looking to achieve/change/improve?
2. What are the goals and objectives for the proposed strategy? The less is more in this case, it is better to have one overarching goal that is contextualized and presents itself as achievable versus five goals that are unachievable. We suggest limiting your goals between one and three for each strategy.

> —Where the goal is defined as a *"desired result/outcome"* over a specified time - Where the objective is defined as *"how you will get there"*
>
> —objectives succinctly describe activities involve in achieving a goal.

3. Describe the strategy and outline specific action steps: who, what, when, how, and so on, and ground these in evidence (cite academic literature, data/analysis, etc.). Although a vision, list of goals and objectives are foundational, it is simply not enough—you must have an actionable plan/steps to guide your progress.

4. What is the expected short-term impact and on which groups (e.g., students/parents, community, staff, etc.)? The short-term expected impact should align with your objective(s).

5. What is the expected long-term impact and on which groups? The long-term expected impact should align with your goal(s) for the strategy.

6. Finally, think through all the structural factors/roadblock that might stand in the way and include ways of addressing these during the implementation.
   - Where the goal is defined as a *"desired result/outcome"* over a specified time.
   - Where the objective is defined as *"how you will get there"*—objectives succinctly describe activities involve in achieving a goal.

As you brainstorm/draft an outline for each strategy, position yourself as an equity-driven leader who is interested in creating a long-lasting change within the context of your chosen school site. We suggest connecting with your peer-review partner(s) after creating an outline for each strategy, and taking turns discussing your outlines, as well as offer and receive feedback.

## Conceptualizing and Drafting a Research Proposal

If you selected research proposal option for a future study or project as your culminating experience, we provide an outline below to get you started. Circle back to your topic, research question(s), and problem statement. Having gone through the exercises of engaging in inquiry throughout this text and knowing what you know now, what would be the next step in advancing the field forward by means of further research? When conceptualizing a research project, in addition to basics such as a well thought-through topic and research questions or hypothesis, a research proposal must address the following three questions:

1. *What do you want to accomplish?* The key in answering this question is clarity and briefness in defining the research problem and it is that you are proposing to investigate/research further.

2. *Why do you want to do the research?* In answering the "why" question, you must address the extant literature and identify gaps that might exist in this literature or if you are proposing a similar study to an investigation that has been done before, explain in what way the results of your study might advance our collective thinking about the topic of investigation/research question. Be sure to answer the "so what?" question (see Chapter 8).

3. *How are you going to conduct the research?* The key element of "how" in the research proposal is your methods section. What method would be most appropriate for the investigation? Within that method, which design do you plan to use? Think of a design as a template to help you unpack your "how." Finally, make sure that what you are proposing is doable and manageable within a proposed timeframe.

4. *What are the potential implications of the study?* When answering this question, you want to talk about impact, impact on the field, research, and so on. In other words, how will your proposed study add to practice and research to move the field forward. Additionally, you also want to discuss potential limitations of your proposed study.

Create an outline as you brainstorm your proposal and think about the method of investigation. Then select the design to help you conceptualize the steps necessary to execute your research. We suggest connecting with your peer-review partner(s) after creating an outline for your research proposal. Take turns discussing your outlines, offering and receiving feedback.

## 12.4 | Conclusion

Irrespective of whether you choose practical direction, research direction, or down the line both—you must always think *for whom* and *because of whom* the educational system exists. You must be mindful and anticipate ahead because without progress, educational system will have no possibility of evolving and an evolution is a necessary component of education. For this and many other reasons, using research as a *tool* will give you a perspective to make better-informed decisions and impact many lives of young people for the better through practices that respect students' humanity and afford them an environment supportive of their strengths.

## 12.5 | Culminating Assignment

Below, we include two culminating assignment templates. You are asked to rely on the work you had done thus far as building blocks for the culminating assignment. For the purposes of concluding this course, we ask that you select either particle or research direction and not both. Of course, you are welcome to circle back to either research proposal or template for practical application and use these as applicable in your future aspirations.

---

**[TEMPLATE FOR PRACTICAL APPLICATION: Final product total word count: 3,500–4,500]**

[TITLE]

### INTRODUCTION

[no more than 300 words]

*This is your chance to frame your work. As you begin to draft your introduction, provide a brief context of the school site, and discuss the school's vision and mission. Then state what drew you to select your chosen state indicator. Finally, remember to unpack your topic and include the research question(s) that guided your work/inquiry as you collected and analyzed quantitative and qualitative data evidence to arrive at the equity gap analysis.*

### QUALITATIVE AND QUANTITATIVE DATA EVIDENCE

**Quantitative Data and Synopsis**
[Insert tables from prior assignments and include synopsis of data; you should have three tables with school site table/data as your main focus, and synopsis should be no more than 500 words]

**Qualitative Data and Synopsis**
[Insert a table of qualitative data description from Chapter 7/Table 4 example and include synopsis of qualitative data; synopsis of data should be no more than 500 words]

**Equity Gap Analysis and A Brief Review of Literature**
[No more than 750 words, see assignment from Chapter 7]

## PROBLEM STATEMENT

[No more than 750 words]

## STRATEGIES FOR SCHOOL IMPROVEMENT

[No more than 350 words per strategy—limit to three strategies; each strategy must be grounded in evidence and provide an outline to address the equity gap]

## References

[Include a list of references here]

---

**[TEMPLATE FOR RESEARCH PROPOSAL: Final product total word count: 3,500–4,500]**

[TITLE]

## INTRODUCTION

[No more than 500 words]

*Your introduction is the "WHAT" question: What do you want to accomplish? This is your chance to frame your proposal. As you begin to draft your introduction, provide a brief summary of the extant literature related to your topic and state how your proposed research project will attempt to fill in the gap in the extant literature. State and unpack the research question(s) you aim to answer or hypothesis you intend to pose as part of your future study. Importantly, unpack ways your proposed research attempts to expand upon our collective knowledge about the topic and/or what impact your proposed research project will have on practice.*

## REVIEW OF LITERATURE

[No more than 1,500 words]

*The review of literature is your "WHY" question: Why do you want to do the research?*

## PRIOR EXAMINATION AND EQUITY GAP ANALYSIS

[No more than 1,000 words]

*This section could create a powerful case for your proposed study.*

*That is, often research proposals include a "pilot" to justify a need for a more extensive study or a similar project to examine other angles on a similar topic. Since you engaged in an examination on a smaller scale, this is your chance to present and discuss the evidence you found thus far to make a stronger case for the study you are proposing.*

## PROBLEM STATEMENT

[No more than 750 words]

*Include your problem statement here.*

## METHODS

[No more than 750 words]

*The methods section is your "HOW" section: How are you going to conduct the research? Include your selected methodology and select the design for your proposed study; discuss why the methodology and design are the best methods to answer the research question you pose. Include subsections as applicable and listed below.*

**Research Question/Hypothesis**

**Researcher's Positionality**

**Population of Focus**

**Research Design**

**Data and Data Analysis**

**Procedure**

## STUDY IMPLICATIONS

[No more than 200 words]

*The implication of the study section is your "SO WHAT?" question: This is your opportunity to stress the potential impact of your proposed project on the field and/or practice. You also want to discuss possible limitations.*

## References

[Include a list of references here]

Milton Keynes UK
Ingram Content Group UK Ltd.
UKHW051943251023
431338UK00007B/56